ALU

AN ADVANCED GUIDE TO OPERATIVE RUNOLOGY

ALU

AN ADVANCED GUIDE TO OPERATIVE RUNOLOGY

A New Handbook of Runes
from the Author of *Futhark*

Edred Thorsson

WEISERBOOKS
San Francisco, CA / Newburyport, MA

First published in 2012 by
Red Wheel/Weiser, LLC
With offices at:
665 Third Street, Suite 400
San Francisco, CA 94107
www.redwheelweiser.com

ISBN: 978-1-57863-526-9

Library of Congress Cataloging-in-Publication Data available upon request

Cover design by Jim Warner
Cover image of Thor, son of Odin. God of thunder shown wielding his
hammer, symbolizing thunder and lightning.
Interior by Kathryn Sky-Peck
Typeset in Sabon

Printed in the United States of America
MAL

10 9 8 7 6 5 4 3 2 1

The paper used in this publication meets the minimum requirements of the
American National Standard for Information Sciences—Permanence of
Paper for Printed Library Materials Z39.48-1992 (R1997).

CONTENTS

List of Tables

PREFACE

It has been well over twenty-five years since the publication of *Futhark: A Handbook of Rune Magic*. Still, this book is not intended to replace or compete with that one—it is intended to go beyond it. This is the first significant advance in the practice of rune-magic to have been published since that time. In fact a world of advancement has been made over the thirty years since the manuscript for *Futhark* was completed. After *Futhark* a myriad of books on rune-magic have appeared—most very bad, some mediocre, and some quite good. But none went beyond the basics. This book will break new ground—theoretically and practically—not just go over the same basic materials one more time. This is also a relatively new kind of book of magic—a text often accompanied by footnotes, references, etc., which bridges the gap between academic runology and "practical magic"—or *operative communication. Alu* is an operative formula which functioned in ancient times as a mode of connecting the realm of the gods to that of humanity. This book is also designed to break through conventional barriers and bring disparate worlds together.

Futhark in many ways is my "worst book"—yet it remains the best selling of my works and has been continuously in print with this publisher since its first appearance in 1984. For those who have not read it, I recommend that you do so before delving into the present work. Versions of *Futhark* evolved from 1975 to 1979, when the final form to be published was fixed. Because at the time runes were virtually unknown in the world of "occult publishing," it took five years for it to see the light of day. The folks who were at Samuel Weiser, Inc. at that time had the courage to bring it out, a spirit which has been extended to the people now working with Red Wheel/Weiser.

But you may ask: how is *Futhark* my "worst book"? There are two answers to that question. First, it is a book full of modern elements (when viewed from an ancient Germanic perspective). These elements were actually taken from the *Armanen* tradition[1] as developed in Germany from the time of Guido von List to Karl Spiesberger. Nothing in the book came from my "imagination." It was all based on the wide-ranging, and sometimes eclectic, early twentieth-century German runic occultism synthesized with what I was just learning about ancient traditions of rune-magic.[2] The second answer is a simple one: One's first book should always be one's worst book! As an author develops himself, so too does his capacity to produce higher-quality work.

Why does *Futhark* remain my most popular book? This is because it partakes to a great extent in the theoretical and practical context of twentieth-century "occultism." It starts where most readers already are in their development. This makes it easier to understand and, hence, more accessible and popular. The same could be said for the volume *Rune Might* (Rûna-Raven, 2004). In the case of *Futhark,* the author was himself not as advanced as he would become—even by the date of the book's original publication—and so it was not overly challenging to the reader. Even at that, many have found *Futhark* to be a breed apart when it comes to works of practical magic in any tradition. This is why you should begin with Futhark—the "ABCs" of the operative runic tradition in our time.

Alu can be a challenging text. Initiates of the Rune-Gild will be well-prepared for its contents. For some others it will be impenetrable—yet for others it will open new doors. Theoretically, *Alu* is based on a purely traditional foundation. Most of the practices discussed are also founded on actual documented operations either within the ancient literature or suggested by archeological or linguistic data, or on evidence of a comparative nature connected to other Indo-European cultures "genetically"[3] related to the Germanic system. Sources for these practices will be documented.[4] This book contains a great number of theoretical constructs and practical techniques never before presented outside a narrow circle. As the work presented here is of an advanced character, I would also strongly recommend that the student acquire and work through the curriculum of the *Nine Doors of Midgard* (Rûna-Raven, 2004, 3rd ed.).

The use of the runes—the system of operative and descriptive semiology of the ancient Germanic peoples—for experiential explorations of the individual soul and the wider multiverse acting as a matrix for that self has a venerable and ancient heritage behind it. "Casting spells" with runes is the necessary youthful adventure of the soul. This book takes students from the upper edge of that youthful experience and guides them to the horizon of wisdom.

Reyn til Rúna!

EDRED THORSSON
WOODHARROW
FEBRUARY 22, 2012

INTRODUCTION

This book is divided into five substantial chapters. The first of these is designed to ground the reader in basic runic knowledge, or runelore. Ideally, the reader will take even more time and effort to study this kind of information in order to gain a deeper understanding in lore before delving beyond this into more practical, or operative, work. The second chapter provides the lore of the individual staves in some new, yet highly traditional, ways. I try to remain as close as possible to the most ancient and original sources for these descriptions of runelore. My personal insights and imaginings are kept to an absolute minimum. There are no "guided" meditations as part of the work here. I think the rune-poems and the other authentic imagery provide more than enough material to ignite the inner vision of individual rune-workers. As theory precedes practice, and understanding comes before speaking, in order to develop as an operative runologist at a higher level, the whole idea of how rune-magic operates, and what the nature of the runes themselves is, needs to be reviewed and revised in the light of greater understanding. Such theoretical material is actually the backbone of all practical advancement. In the third chapter we consider not only traditional theories, but the latest scientific or academic theories about how magic works, and we synthesize these into a radical new vision.

The fourth and fifth chapters are the operative handbook itself. Here we will learn to write the runes. When runes are written, things happen. Methods of carving and scraping runes and the art of sending runic communications in ways that make them effective in the subjective and objective universes are outlined in practical detail. Finally, the topic of carving runestones is approached in a down-to-earth way. This final runic art is the most important and most powerful form of operative runology, and it must be approached with great care. This book provides the instructions readers need to work themselves up to the level where they can actually practice this art in a reliable and authentic way.

Alu has a few features that might be unfamiliar to some readers. First of all, there are quite a few endnotes. These try to explain obscure aspects, point the reader to further information, or provide the source for an idea. Also I have included, where possible, ancient examples of runic evidence. This material is presented in various ways. Original (usually "normalized") runes are often provided. Runes sometimes demonstrated variant forms of their classic normal shapes, and for the sake of clarity I have provided these in their normal forms. The actual runic characters are then usually transcribed (one lower case Roman letter in **boldface** corresponding to one rune as noted in the various tables in the text). The inscriptions may also be transliterated into classic forms of various older Germanic dialects, e.g., Proto-Germanic, Old English, Old Norse, which appear in italics. Finally, translations are provided set off by quotation marks. (These features are standard academic runological practice.) This academic practice is followed so that the aspiring radical operative runologist will more easily be able to make use of scientific material in his or her continuing quest.

The true advanced character of this text is embodied in the prevalent idea that runes and runic texts can be composed in one's own language and applied in an operative, or magical, context. This at once liberates the practitioner from the limits imposed by the use of ancient languages or set formulas, but at the same time challenges magicians to create their own formulas just as the ancient rune-magicians did. With this challenge comes an increased departure from the secure confines of traditional formulas. The magic has to come more from within the magician than from the formulas themselves. For this to work well, a significantly advanced state of initiation is required.

Abbreviations

Dan.	Danish
DR	Danmarks Runeindskrifter (= Jacobsen-Moltke, 1942)
Go.	Gothic
IE	Indo-European
IK	Ikonographischer Katalog
KJ	Edition of the older runic inscriptions by W. Krause and H. Jankuhn (1966)
MHG	Middle High German
OE	Old English
O.Ir.	Old Irish
ON	Old Norse
OERP	Old English Rune-Poem
OHG	Old High German
OIRP	Old Icelandic Rune-Poem
ONRR	Old Norwegian Rune-Rhyme
PGmc.	Proto-Germanic
PIE	Proto-Indo-European
PNorse	Primitive Norse

Note on Transcriptions of Runic Inscriptions and Treatment of Foreign Terms

Runes are transcribed into Roman letters in boldface: ᚠᛚᚢ is transcribed **alu**.

When a runic inscription is transliterated into a known or reconstructed language, the letters are set in italics, so **alu** = *alu*.

Letters between square brackets [. . .] indicate an informal phonetic representation of the sound.

Letters between slash marks / . . . / indicate a representation of a general grapheme, or letter-symbol.

CHAPTER ONE

GROUNDING IN KNOWLEDGE

Before galdor (magic) can be worked at the highest levels, a great deal of knowledge must be gained. The highest aim of magic is wisdom, or true understanding. In order to understand, one must first absorb a certain mass of knowledge—much of it "theoretical"—which must be put into practice. In practice, theoretical knowledge is realized, experience gained, and being is elevated. From this elevated, or "risen up," perspective of consciousness, when one's Æsiric intelligence is—even if only for a few moments—realized, one is fully capable of divine acts. It is also true that one must begin with basic things before advanced things can be considered, much less attempted. This only makes good sense. Balance in development is essential.

Let's start here by defining a few very basic terms in ways that lead to the construction of a personal frame of reference which is conducive to the working of galdor. We will also survey briefly the origins of the runes—their mythic and historical roots, the various historical epochs in which they were consulted, and the verifiable uses the runes have been put to in the past. This story of the runes is concluded by a brief discussion of the runic revival, which has been going on intermittently since the seventeenth century.

One of the essential tasks not only of this book, but all of operative runology, is that of guiding personal transformation. An important feature often ignored in schools of "magic" is the necessity of an initial paradigm shift in the individual. That is, the frame of reference, the basic "operating myth"—however one would like to express the fact that each person operates from within some theoretical framework—must be altered in a way that makes galdor possible and beneficial. If one remains entirely within the consensus reality of the modern world, magic is relatively impossible. The modern world is dominated by a materialistic, rationalistic (positivistic) model. This myth (and it is a myth, as are all such frames of reference) works like a machine or organism—outside of which nothing exists. Such a myth restricts the divine acts of galdormen and gods. However, the eternal traditional myth of the world embraced by our ancestors and their ancestors actually enhances the possibility of magic. Different things are possible in different worlds. The very word "world" contains an ancient Germanic concept "a man's (wer-) age (old)."[5] As a term it takes into account the idea of the "world" being conditioned by thought—the chief distinguishing activity of men and gods. The process of conducting this shift in frame of reference can happen mysteriously and suddenly for a very few—but more often long, hard work at a high level of consciousness is what is needed. This is done by exposing oneself to the traditional lore of our ancestors, listening to what wise people have said about this lore through the centuries, learning the ancient dialects (Old Norse, Old English), and undertaking a curriculum of exercises such as those found in the *Nine Doors of Midgard*. As a practical matter, it has also been found that personal contact with those who have made the "shift" is essential to traditional work.

Definitions

Among the elements necessary to the formation of an effective and true frame of reference, the definition of certain key words is an important start. The definitions of some of these terms are often vague rather than sharp around their "edges." This allows them to slide from one meaning to another over time. By the same token, we can, with knowledge and effort, slide them back to meanings of a more archaic, and often more potent and useful, level.

In any case, the advanced operative runologist will not remain content with studying the ancient lore in translation, but will endeavor to learn the most important ancient Germanic dialects in order to crack the subtle code of the archaic frame of reference. However, even depending on more "dictionary definitions" of ancient words can be slightly misleading. For example, if you translate the Old Norse word *ørlög* with the modern English word "fate" in reading a text in Old Norse, you have simply substituted a familiar (mis)conception for an unfamiliar word. Key terms must be studied in depth and understood in their ancient context, and their etymologies must be studied and understood as well.[6]

In order to build up a traditional frame of reference, one must study hundreds of words in context. Among the most important books for this exercise is the seminal *Culture of the Teutons* by Vilhelm Grönbech.[7] Our present study is, however, devoted to the advanced practice of operative runology and cannot delve too deeply into this necessary prerequisite to such practice. But we will need to clarify certain terms before proceeding.

RUNIC ROOTS

By now most are familiar with the idea that the word "rune" (PGmc. *rūnō*) did not mean a "letter" or "character," but rather a *mystery* or *secret*. Here we want to go beyond this mere definition to discover the real essence of the word. To do this requires a significant contextual understanding of the word in ancient times. In a forthcoming monograph, *Rūn-: The Investigation of an Etymon*, I will more fully explore all of the ramifications of this term.

The simple definition as "mystery" or "secret" stems from the uses found in all the major older Germanic dialects. There we find ON *rún* "secret lore" (and perhaps also "words or songs");[8] OE *rūn* "secret, mystery, a whisper, secret council";[9] OHG *rūna* "mystery";[10] OS *rūna* "secret council" and *girūni* "secret"; Go. *rūna*, which translates both "mystery" and "council."[11] There are consistent links between the idea of "mystery" and secret communication or vocal performance (e.g., "whispering"). This field of meaning is supported by the ultimate derivation of the word from PIE *reu-* "to roar, bellow." Still, this etymology may or may not be correct. The actual word is not found outside of Germanic and Celtic languages.[12] Therefore it may be a Celto-Germanic isogloss; in other words, a term unique to these languages. The Proto-Germanic word *rūnō* is found in the older runic inscriptions perhaps as many as sixteen times. We find it used both in the singular, e.g., on the fourth-century stone of Einang (Norway): . . . *dag[s]tiR rūnō fahidō* ("[I, . . . dagast colored the rune"), and in the plural, e.g., the gold bracteate of Tjurkö I from about 450 CE (IK 184): *wurtē rūnō R an walhakurnē* ("the runes are worked on Welsh grain [= gold]").[13] In both instances, the word clearly indicates the product of the runemaster's craft, whether for the whole inscription (seen as a mystery in the singular) or the individual signs (in the plural). From what we already know, we can say with great certainty that the runes are visible symbolic manifestations of a (vocal) communicative act. The contextual discussions below will help us realize the mysterious quality they possess.[14]

One of the main ways the ancient Germanic dialects created new words (and hence expressed different concepts) was by way of stem vowel mutation. In this way a seed of meaning—in our example, *rūn-* "mystery"—could be spread within its perceived wider semantic field to produce new words/concepts with a sometimes hidden link to their original forms. These stem vowel mutations did not occur arbitrarily, however. There are certain rules or parameters within which this process works. The two main inventories of such variations are known as the *ablaut series* (by which strong verbs such as "sing, sang, sung" are developed) and the phenomenon called *umlaut*.[15]

By taking the stem vowel in the word *ru_n-* and subjecting it to these mutations, a variety of new words/concepts emerge. These can best be verified and observed in Old Norse where we find the following examples: *Rún* (with *ablaut*) —> *raun*: "trial, experiment, experience." *Raun* (with i-*umlaut*) —> *reyna*: "to try; examine; search, pry into." *Rún* (with i-*umlaut*) —> *rýna*: "to inquire, pry into." Additionally, there is another word which seems related: *ræna*: "consciousness."[16] Already a strong semantic field has developed around the meanings of these derivatives. Clearly the seed concept contained in *ru_n-* not only emphasizes the unknown, but also the means and ways of making the unknown known: *A mystery pried into leads to experience which becomes awareness.* This does not exhaust the possibilities of the discussion, but space prevents me from delving deeper at this time.[17]

Besides this method of stem vowel shifting, Germanic dialects also broadly used the more familiar modes of adding prefixes and suffixes or other words in compounds to stems to create new or expanded meanings. In Old Norse, for example, we find *rún-* suffixed with weak masculine and feminine endings, *rúni* and *rúna*, respectively, to produce words meaning "secret advisor or counselor," be that advisor male or female. One of the ways the original name of the Rune-Gild, *Rúnagildi*, could be interpreted is "guild of secret advisors," not necessarily "guild of the runes." The stem *reyn-* also receives suffixes to produce *reyn-sla*: "experience"; *reyn-d*: "experience" (used in the genitive case *reyndar*, to mean "in fact"); and *reynir*: "trier, examiner."

Another way that the meaning of the word *rūn-* was expanded upon was through the more familiar method of combining or compounding it with another word or with suffixes. Both Old English and Old Norse are rich in such words. In Old English, for example, we find *rūnnwita*: "confidant, councilor, sage"; *rūnncofa*: "mind"; and *hellerūnne*: "sorceress." This last term is a combination of the feminine suffixed form of *rūn*, with the word for "the realm of the dead"—*hell*. This combination is extremely old, as it appears in Jordanes's *History of the Goths,* where he uses the word *haljarunae*,[18] which reflects the original Gothic term **haljarunos*. These are said to be the Gothic sorceresses who mated with baleful forest spirits to give birth to the Huns! In Old Norse there is a catalog of compound runic words given in the Sigrdrífumál. There we find, among others, *málrúnar*: "speech runes"; *bjargrúnar*: "birth-runes"; *gaman-rúnar*: "pleasure-runes"; *sigrúnar*: "victory runes"; *ölrúnar*: ale-runes." This last term is of particular interest to us here because etymologically it is derived from **alu-rūnoz* and as we will see, Old Norse öl: "ale" comes from PNorse *alu*.

From this brief survey it can be seen that the root word *rūn-* clearly belongs to a sacred and sometimes "magical"—or operative—semantic field.[19] Its vital and vigorous usages in both Old Norse and Old English show that it was a much thought about and revered concept. Its application to "written character" is obviously secondary, but also shows the intrinsic value placed on the act of writing itself by the Germanic peoples who first became familiar with the runes. No doubt the term *rūn-*

was in use long before the development of the *fuþark*. Both Old English and Old Norse use the term "stave," *stæf* or *stafr*, respectively, when referring specifically to the concrete, visible sign of a rune. (With time the words *stæf* or *stafr* take on some of the more "mysterious" or "magical" qualities originally reserved for the word *rún*.) *Rūnō* is, in its original sense, a mystery (μυστηριον): something hidden, unknown. The contemplation of the very concept of the unknown is a powerful catalyst for the generation of power, knowledge, and even wisdom. All knowing begins with a sense of the unknown . . .[20]

Reyn til Rúna!

: ᚱᛖᛃᚾ ᛏᛁᛚᚱᚢᚾᚪᛃ :

MAGIC

Ancient Germanic tradition is extremely rich in terms for what might be roughly translated as "magic."[21] To define magic in the totality of the scope of those terms and the historical practices they reflect goes beyond what we need to address here. We are concerned with that kind of magic that involves, or can involve, the use of the runes.

All forms of magic, and especially magic using runes, are modes of communication. What is essential is that the magician, or operator, knows the code and is able to execute the code in an effective manner in order that the return message will be in keeping with the intention of the operator.[22]

Old Norse and Old English words for "magic" often convey the idea of special knowledge and performance of a code. The most common term, and one of the most often linked to runic activities, is ON *galdr* (OE *gealdor*). We have "modernized" this word as "galdor." Etymologically, it goes back to the verb *gala*, which denotes the sound a raven or crow makes. In this there is a deep mythic connection to the god Óðinn/Wóden, who is served by two ravens: Huginn and Muninn (the one who *thinks* and the one who *remembers*, respectively). For ages magical incantations—*galdrar*—were only sung or chanted. With the advent of the runes, suddenly the operator could make his incantations—already poetic and/or rhythmic utterances harmonious with divine forms—even closer to the essence of the divine world because they could be made more permanent and more perfect.

Other ancient terms for magic emphasize the special knowledge needed by the operator: ON *fjölkyngi* and *forneskja*[23] are two of these. *Fjölkyngi* refers to knowledge which is deep, manifold, complex. This special knowledge enables an operator to communicate effectively with unseen, yet powerful forces and entities in the environment. *Forneskja* specifically indicates the idea that magical knowledge is ancient. Although this latter term became more prevalent in the Christian era, pointing to the idea that magical knowledge was specifically heathen, the term could also have been used in pre-Christian times since for the Germanic peoples the idea of the ancient, mythical past is always linked to the eternal value of these mythic ideals and patterns.

Radical runologists are those who have no inner conflict between objective and subjective definitions. As a radical runologist, or "rune-magician," one should not be baffled by the scholarly discussion of magic (from an anthropological perspective) nor should the scholarly definition of magic be one which does not take into account the cultural and philosophical validity and reality of the practice of magic in societies of all kinds.[24] In my article on "Magic" in *Medieval Scandinavia: An Encyclopedia,* I defined the topic as "volitive symbolic behavior to effect or prevent changes in the environment by means of extraordinary communicative acts with paranormal factors."[25] This definition works for both a scholarly (anthropological) discussion as well as for a practical, or applied, purpose. This definition must, however, be studied word for word and completely understood intellectually. We will periodically return to theoretical considerations, for in order for one to be effective, one must possess and understand a firm theoretical model. (Most modern people's "magic" has little chance of success because they generally lack a firm and complete model.)

Before leaving these opening definitions to move on to the historical framework of the runes, I must say something about the word that provides the title of this book: *Alu*. The runic formula *alu* appears in well over twenty of the older runic inscriptions.[26] It represents the Germanic word *alu*, which gives us our modern "ale." In ancient times words which represented substances of extreme symbolic importance were used either in conjunction with the substance in ritual settings or as symbolic substitutes for the substances themselves. As early as 1954, Edgar Polomé pointed to the etymological connection between *alu* and Hittite *alwanza-* (*alwanzatar*: "witchcraft, magic, spell"; *alwanza*: "to bewitch").[27] It appears prominently in the corpus of bracteate[28] texts—which are categorically magical in character as the objects represent amulets or religious medals. *Alu* reflects a word which originally described a religious or mystical state of mind, which was semantically transferred to a substance (fermented drink) used in religious and magical ritual. *Alu* becomes öl in Old Norse (see *ölrúnar* above). Because *alu* so often comes at the end of magico-religious formulas, it seems rather clear that that it was a verbal-symbolic formula used to conclude a sacred or magically potent utterance and that it has the effect of sanctifying (or "loading") the foregoing words—just as sacrificial ale could be poured on a stone to sanctify it in religious ceremonies, which is especially known from funerary rites.

In terms of numerical symbolism,[29] it is also noteworthy that ᚨᛚᚢ = 4.21.2 = 27 (= 3 × 9 : 2 + 7 = 9) and ON öl (spelled runically ᛏᚢᚱ in the Younger Futhark) = 10.2.15 = 27! This standard numerical lore would indicate that ᚠᚢᚾ is a trebling of 9. Using the Uþark code,[30] ᚠᚢᚾ = 3.20.1 = 24—a *pars pro toto* sign of the whole fuþark.

As "magic" is a form of inter-reality communication—between humans and gods, between mind and nature, etc.—the runes provide a traditional and traditionally perfect metalanguage for this form of communication, or operative performance. The highest aims of present-day rune-magic would mirror those of ancient times—but the possibilities of results for lower forms of rune-magic are conditioned by what is *necessary* now versus what was *necessary* then. The highest aims of rune-magic today are twofold: 1) self-completion (initiation) and 2) restoration of our tradition.

Runic History

In order to be able to work with a rich, complex, and authentic tradition, it is highly desirable to be as familiar as possible with its various manifestations over time. These manifestations should be viewed from various perspectives, e.g., from within and from without. That is, from within its own mythology, or traditional self-understanding, and from an objective point of view supported by data and reasonable theories. For one who wishes to practice operative runology at the highest levels, no stone should be left unturned—or unexamined! Knowing the history of a system helps the practitioner by showing him what was done in the past as a way of giving some shape to what is possible today. In this book I will touch on many questions of history, but since the focus of our explorations is not history, such explorations are more completely discussed in other works.[31]

ORIGINS

If one understands the origin of something, one can possess great power with regard to that thing. When we speak of runes, we speak of two different, yet intimately related things: 1) the idea of the Mystery as articulated by twenty-four visible signs, and 2) the idea of twenty-four visible signs (staves) used to represent the sounds of a spoken language.

In the traditional world of more than a thousand years ago, these two aspects would have formed parts of a coherent whole—which is what the radical runologist strives for today. However, in order to arrive at the highest level of understanding, one must often delve into the polar extremes of a topic.[32] An imbalanced view—weighted too much in the objective or too much in the subjective direction—will quickly run our wagon right into a ditch.

Mythic Origin of the Runes

"Myth" is a word that has come to mean a "lie" in the muddled modernistic mindset. Actually a myth is not something untrue, but rather it conveys something so deeply true and real that mere facts are too particular and small to contain it. Myth is always True—and therefore can never be contained by history. History—like literature—is only really significant when it in some small measure reflects, no matter how imperfectly, mythic reality. Because of the overriding validity of myth, especially when it touches on the understanding of things belonging to a traditional culture, we must address the myth of runic origins before we look at the mundane historical facts. Myth is made up of eternally remembered forms—stored images and formulas which can be recalled by the soul—especially in times of Need (= psychological stress). Science is the logical, cognitive process of analyzing and interpreting data so that it can "make sense" and be of use to the conscious mind. In Grímnismál 20, Óðinn speaks to these two structures in terms of his ravens, Muninn (he who remembers) and Huginn (he who thinks):

> *Huginn ok Muninn*　　　　　　*fljúga hverjan dag*
> 　　　　*jörmungrund yfir;*
> *óomk ek of Hugin,*　　　　　　*at hann aptr né komið,*
> 　　　　*þó sjámk meirr um Munin.*

> Huginn and Muninn　　　　　　fly every day
> 　　　　over the expansive earth;
> I am anxious about Huginn,　　that he will not come back,
> 　　　　though I fear even more for Muninn.

Here we see that Óðinn treasures Muninn over Huginn because without *memory* mere *thinking* is devoid of meaning.

When we look at the myth of the origin of the runes contained in Hávamál stanzas 138–45, we gain a glimpse into the traditional manner of thinking. If we could go back to say the year 800, and speak to a living, traditionally trained, runemaster, we could ask him: "Where did the runes come from?" His answer would certainly be something closely akin in content to what we read in this text found within the *Poetic Edda*, also called the "Rúnatals þáttr Óðins" (The Story of Odin's List of Runes/Mysteries) [= Hávamál stanzas 138–65].[33]

Structurally this text, as far as runic origins are concerned, begins with the god Óðinn describing how he is hung *up* in a tree—suspended above the world. From this sacrificial position—the typical Odinic sacrifice was one in which the victim was hung in a tree and stabbed with a spear[34]—Óðinn slips toward death (Hel). At the moment just before death, however, he confronts (and is suddenly informed by) the great Mystery (*Rúna*). She pours all of herself into him wholly. He is shocked back to Life! He overcomes Death and falls *down* again to the world. Here we have the typical structure of *all* initiatory or transformational rites:

I: Separation—hanging up

II: Transformation—reception of Rúna

III: Reinclusion—falling back down

Óðinn has received the great Mystery, and in it there is an implicit structure or formula which makes it intelligible to the mind. The complete ineffable Mystery—as a whole beyond the capacity of language or even thought to capture—is articulated or analyzed into a symbolic structure: originally twenty-four visible signs representing twenty-four sounds in a certain order, each sign possessed of a culturally symbolic name and the system divided into three groups of eight signs.

The poem then variously recounts ways in which Óðinn declares himself able to read the runes—to understand the mysteries he sought after and, what is more, to be able to write (carve) them. His knowledge is not only passive, but active as well. He understands as a philosopher would like to understand, but he also creates and modifies the world with his knowledge. One of the main ways in which the All-Father uses the runes to modify the world is by teaching their use to certain humans. These were the original guild of runemasters focused on the cult of Óðinn and on the use of their knowledge for the deep enhancement of their traditions through conscious awareness— the gift of Wōðanaz-Wiljōn-Wīhaz.

The "Rúnatals þáttr Óðins" provides all we need to know about the traditional origins of the runes in the realm of the gods and in the realm of the human soul. However, further objective knowledge helps guide us in the here and now to understand the mysteries of the runes more powerfully.

Historical Origins

The traditional mythic origins of the runes provide inner knowledge, but the historical origin of the runestaves orients us in mundane tradition in a way that completes and grounds our understanding. Those who lack a firm foundation in historical knowledge about the runes often find themselves wandering in an intellectual wasteland, having lost their bearings in this world—and it is in this world we must truly begin our journey.

Objective history concerning the runestaves—writing with runes—begins with the oldest runic evidence (perhaps as early as the middle of the first century CE) coupled with comparative evidence drawn from the history of the development of writing systems and their introduction into various cultures.[35] There is a general principle used by some historians of writing that the time of the actual origin of a system dates back some one to two hundred years before the first surviving hard evidence for the system. (This is due to the fact that early efforts are often on perishable objects.) The oldest possible runic inscription is on the brooch of Meldorf, 46 CE.[36] Therefore, using our general principle, the date of runic origins in the Germanic world would be around 150 to 50 BCE.

The idea that runes were invented in isolation in the north and that they date back to some primeval time (e.g., that of "Atlantis"), or that they are the origins of all writing,[37] is untenable on historical, linguistic, and archeological grounds.

Clearly the Germanic peoples got the idea of writing in general from some literate culture to their south. Historically, three different writing systems have been proposed—all ultimately derived from the tradition of writing originating among the Phoenicians around 1000 BCE. The three candidates for the model used by the creator of the runic system are: the Greek, North-Italic (or Etruscan), and Roman. I will not go into the histories of these scripts here.[38]

Early in the scientific study of the runes many scholars sentimentally favored the Greek origin.[39] This sentiment was driven by the prestige of Hellenism, coupled with the idealization of the Goths, the Germanic tribe that first made contact with Hellas. This, however, did not fit the historical and archeological data, as the Germanic peoples had little to no direct contact with the Greeks before around 200 CE, although amber was traded southward from the Baltic as early as Mycenaean times (1600–1150 BCE). Additionally, the Greek letters do not match very well with the runes typologically. The North-Italic scripts (used in the alpine regions of what are now northern Italy, Switzerland, and Austria) would seem to be the best historical/geographical fit, since Germanic peoples would have come into contact with this alphabet early on in their ventures southward. There are even two inscriptions in a Germanic dialect on helmets (Negau A and B) using a North-Italic script.[40] However, once more the typological correlation between the shapes and sound-values of the runes and the North-Italic characters is very poor. (One modern occult writer on the runes even erroneously and repeatedly identified a North-Italic script as the "runic alphabet" itself!) The best historical fit seems to be offered by the Roman (Latin) alphabet. Shape/sound-value correlations such as: ᚠ:F, ᚢ:U, ᚱ:R, ᚺ:H, ᛁ:I, ᛋ:S, ᛏ:T, ᛒ:B, ᛗ:M, ᛚ:L, ᛟ:O are hard to explain away otherwise. The objection that the Romans were far removed from the Germanic peoples at the time of the genesis of the runic system can be overcome by the existence of early mercantile contacts and trade routes between Rome and Germania. Also the timing of the probable origin of the runic writing system more or less correlates with the age of the earliest foray of the Germanic tribes known as the Cimbri and Teutones into the environs of Roman Europe in the late second century BCE.

All evidence points to the runes first being used in Scandinavia—not in lands bordering the Roman world. The most likely scenario is this: A Germanic chieftain (and "priest") with historical ties (through trade, war, or both) to the Roman world became marginally literate in Roman letters. He innovatively applied this knowledge, synthesized with his own native Germanic sense of symbology, to fashion the runic system of writing. This process was, for him, not divorced from a sense of awe and mystery. Nor was this sense lost on those few to whom he taught the system. Clearly this was a man of great prestige—or he won such prestige due to the power of his inspired creation. The fact that his system survived for hundreds of years and was used by members of a dozen tribes different from his own is a clear and objective testimony to the power and prestige of the system.[41]

HISTORY OF THE RUNESTAVES

The runestaves can be mapped historically in a couple of significant ways. The use of runes in writing systems can be laid out chronologically. There we see that the runic system underwent a successive series of developments, each phase of which lasted several hundred years. To a certain extent we can also analyze the use of runes in various types of inscriptions. The runes are implicitly a system for communication. The contents of these communicative acts can therefore be broken down and discussed historically.[42]

Prehistory

From the speculation concerning the origin of the runes already given, it can be guessed that the individual who developed the system was already familiar with some symbols or ideographs—but not with writing in the conventional sense. The idea that the runes in toto "evolved" out of more primitive ideographs is untenable for reasons already given relating to the Roman alphabet. However, it is likely that certain runes were related to such ideographs, runes which represented sounds which to the Germanic ear the Roman alphabet offered no equivalent, e.g., ᛞ, ᚹ, ᛃ, ᛊ, ᛉ, ᛜ. Also the tradition of ascribing names to the runes suggests a close relationship between the original idea of what the runes were and the older tradition of iconic symbols, i.e., symbols which stood for images. That a sign should have a name, e.g., ᚷ = *gēbō*: "gift," would naturally lead the individual to look for some sort of link between the visible sign and some visual association or abstract meaning evoked by the name. Such speculations were common enough among other ancient peoples such as the Greeks and Hebrews.[43]

From the beginning, there were twenty-four runes. They constitute what is called the Older Fuþark. The system appeared as shown in Table 1.1.

Table 1.1: The Older Fuþark System

1	2	3	4	5	6	7	8
ᚠ	ᚢ	ᚦ	ᚨ	ᚱ	ᚲ	ᚷ	ᚹ
f	u	þ	a	r	k	g	w
fehu	*ūruz*	*þurisaz*	*ansuz*	*raiðō*	*kēnaz*	*gēbō*	*wunjō*
"cattle"	"aurochs"	"giant"	"god"	"ride"	"torch"	"gift"	"joy"
9	10	11	12	13	14	15	16
ᚺ	ᚾ	ᛁ	ᛃ	ᛇ	ᛈ	ᛉ	ᛊ
h	n	i	j	ei	p	R	s
hagalaz	*nauþiz*	*īsa*	*jēra*	*eihwaz*	*perþrō*	*elhaz*	*sowilō*
"hail"	"need"	"ice"	"year"	"yew"	"pear"	"elk"	"sun"
17	18	19	20	21	22	23	24
ᛏ	ᛒ	ᛖ	ᛗ	ᛚ	ᛜ	ᛞ	ᛟ
t	b	e	m	l	ng	d	o
tīwaz	*berkanō*	*ehwaz*	*mannaz*	*laguz*	*ingwaz*	*dagaz*	*ōþila*
"Tyr"	"birch goddess"	"horse"	"man"	"water"	"Ing"	"day"	"estate"

This system was in use from the genesis of the runes to around the year 750 CE. The bulk of the inscriptions found in the Older Fuþark are in what are today the Scandinavian countries. There are a few (about ten) Older Fuþark inscriptions scattered here and there over eastern Europe where the Germanic peoples were migrating, and there are around seventy inscriptions found in what is today Germany, almost all of which date from the sixth to seventh centuries. In all, there are some 500 Older Fuþark inscriptions—half of this number is accounted for in the vast corpus of bracteate inscriptions.[44]

At about the time of the migration of a number of Angles, Saxons, and Jutes from the North Sea coast of Europe to the southern and eastern parts of Britain, there occurred an innovation in the runic system used by these tribes and the Frisians, who for the most part remained in the ancestral homeland in present-day Holland and northwestern Germany. Their innovation, historically typical of the development of other alphabets, consisted of *adding* signs to the system as their language developed sounds for which the original system had no sign. So around the time of 500 CE, we begin to see evidence for the so-called Anglo-Frisian Fuþorc. It did not emerge as a complete system immediately, but seems to have evolved slowly. At least by the late fifth century, there were twenty-eight or twenty-nine runes in the system (which were used in the bulk of the inscriptions), but later even more were added (mostly only seen in runic *manuscripts*) until a total of thirty-three runes were in some sort of use. These are shown in Table 1.2.

The active use of this system for inscriptions ceased sometime during the eleventh century. Geographically, inscriptions were limited to England and Frisia. However, it was also recorded widely in manuscripts produced by English monks in monasteries on the continent of Europe.

Meanwhile in Scandinavia there occurred a runic revolution. The actual language represented by the runic inscriptions—vari-

Table 1.2: The Anglo-Frisian Fuþorc

1	2	3	4	5	6	7	8	
ᚠ	ᚢ	ᚦ	ᚩ	ᚱ	ᚳ	ᚷ	ᚹ	
f	u	þ	o	r	k	g	w	
feoh	*ūr*	*þorn*	*ōs*	*rād*	*ċēn*	*gyfū*	*wynn*	
"cattle"	"aurochs"	"thorn"	"god"	"ride"	"torch"	"gift"	"joy"	

9	10	11	12	13	14	15	16	
ᚻ	ᚾ	ᛁ	ᛄ	ᛇ	ᛈ	ᛉ	ᛋ	
h	n	i	j	ei	p	x	s	
hæġl	*nȳd*	*īs*	*ġēr*	*eoh*	*perðrō*	*eolhx*	*siġel*	
"hail"	"need"	"ice"	"year"	"yew"	"pear"	"elk"	"sun"	

17	18	19	20	21	22	23	24	
ᛏ	ᛒ	ᛖ	ᛗ	ᛚ	ᛝ	ᛞ	ᛟ	
t	b	e	m	l	ng	d	œ	
tīr	*beorc*	*eh*	*mann*	*lagu*	*Ing*	*dæġ*	*œþel*	
"glory"	"birch"	"horse"	"man"	"water"	"Ing"	"day"	"estate"	

25	26	27	28	29	30	31	32	33
ᚪ	ᚫ	ᚣ	ᛡ	ᛠ	ᛢ	ᛣ	ᛥ	ᛤ
a	æ	y	io	ea	q	c [k]	st	g
āc	*æsc*	*ȳr*	*ior*	*ēar*	*cweorð*	*calc*	*stān*	*gār*
"oak"	"ash"	"yew bow"	"eel"	"earth"	"fire-whisk"	"chalice"	"stone"	"spear"

ous dialects of Old Norse—was becoming ever more complex as far as the number of different sounds it possessed. The normal reaction given this circumstance is for an alphabet to expand to accommodate the new sounds. Instead, around 750, some individual, or a highly organized group of men,[45] transformed the runic system into the sixteen-rune Younger Fuþąrk. Thus, contrary to the expected development, they reduced the number of signs. The new system is shown in Table 1.3.

Table 1.3: The Younger Fuþąrk

1	2	3	4	5	6
ᚠ	ᚢ	ᚦ	ᚬ	ᚱ	ᚴ
fé	*úr*	*þurs*	*áss*	*reið*	*kaun*
"wealth"	"drizzle"	"giant"	"god"	"ride"	"sore"
7	8	9	10	11	
ᚼ	ᚾ	ᛁ	ᛆ	ᛋ	
hagall	*nauð*	*íss*	*ár*	*sól*	
"hail"	"need"	"ice"	"good year"	"sun"	
12	13	14	15	16	
ᛏ	ᛒ	ᛘ	ᛚ	ᛣ	
týr	*bjarkan*	*maðr*	*lögr*	*ýr*	
"Týr"	"birch"	"man"	"water"	"yew bow"	

The exact reasons for the reduction of the runes from twenty-four to sixteen remain a mystery. Scholarly speculation ranges from a simplification for ease of learning to an obfuscation of their system of writing in the face of an ideological onslaught from Christianity. At this point I think that it is most likely that the system was made more difficult and obscure (through simplification) because various "noninitiates" outside the guild of runemasters had perhaps become familiar with the older system such that they could actually read the inscriptions made in that system. As we will see later, it is likely that the ancient runemasters only wanted their inscriptions to be read by a certain limited and elite group of individuals.

The system of the Younger Fuþąrk continued in its pure form for about four hundred years. Around 1150 there started to appear so-called dotted or pointed runestaves which helped account for the signs lost in the revision of the older system. Thus ᚴ, which stood for both /k/ and /g/ (as well as /ng/) appeared as a "pointed" stave ᚵ for /g/ and remained unpointed (ᚴ) for /k/. Over the years this developed into a virtual "runic alphabet," which means that there was a distinctive runestave for each letter of the modified Latin alphabet as used to write the medieval Scandinavian dialects. Although this system was used for writing and carving runes, knowledge of the fuþąrk system of sixteen runes did not die out, as the many **fuþąrk** inscriptions of the Middle Ages show. Only very rarely was the runic alphabet, as shown in Table 1.4, employed in its ordered entirety as any sort of magical formula, as was so common for the **fuþąrk**.[46]

Table 1.4: The Runic Alphabet

ᚼ	B	ı	↑	ᚠ	ᛈ	ᛈ	✳	I	ᛈ	ᚱ	Ψ	ᚼ
a	b	c	d	e	f	g	h	i/j	k	l	m	n
ᚼ	B	ᛈ	R	ᚼ	Þ	↑	∩	ᚼ	ı	✝	✝	
o	p	q	r	s	þ	t	u	y	z	æ	ö	

Runes continued to be used in one capacity or another by country folk in remote regions of Sweden until the nineteenth century. But clearly the old socio-cultic structure which had originated and carried the runes forth in history from their beginnings waned under the progressive influence of Christian institutions. This is not to say that the early Christians of Scandinavia were immediately hostile to runes. A vast number of the greatest runestones of Sweden from the eleventh century are of ostensibly Christian content and often display Christian icons, such as the cross. However, it might be convincingly argued that the very motivation and long tradition of the carving of such stones remained essentially traditional (i.e., heathen).

HISTORICAL USES OF THE RUNES

Our knowledge about the historical uses of the runes stems from the contents of the inscriptions themselves, coupled with archeological and comparative data, including information gleaned from literary sources in Old Norse and Old English. Although some current academic runologists argue that the runes were a script like any other and were thought to have no intrinsic "magical" qualities, it can be observed that no inscription in the Older Fuþark can be shown to be unambiguously profane or to have served an "ordinary" function entirely divorced from connotations of the holy. Only in the Christian Middle Ages do such obviously profane inscriptions begin to appear.

Through the centuries runes served every sort of purpose, from magical incantations to owner's marks on tools. However, a historical analysis clearly shows that the sacred predominated in the early phases, with profane uses growing as the integral pagan Germanic culture was progressively compromised by the Christianization process. Still, the vast majority of literary references, for example in Old Norse sagas and poems, show that in the medieval mind runes were primarily used for mysterious purposes, or were even still equated with the idea of esoteric lore. Additionally, many of the poems were being written at the same time that some of the most important and symbolically elaborate runestones were being carved.

Here we will concentrate on the magical or operative use of runes in ancient times. Often there is an operative dimension to what appears to be an "ordinary" inscription, or one which does not seem at first glance to be overtly magical or religious. A survey of some of the more conspicuous magical motivations for ancient runic inscriptions includes:

- Preventing the walking dead

- Protection from harm

- Acquiring love (romantic love)

- Prosperity and health

- Cursing enemies or evildoers

- Sanctifying objects

- Objectifying inner psychological states

- Memorialization

- Immortalization

It must be remembered that the ancient inscriptions were executed in a traditional time and the concerns and motivations of runemasters then were different from what they need to be now. Our aims and theirs are the same, but our operations are different because we live in a different sort of world. Theirs was traditional; ours is post-traditional. Their aim was most often to maintain their timeless ways; ours is to recover what has been lost.

Returning to the list of nine operative motivations above, let us discuss each in order to clarify the magical universe in which the traditional runemasters operated.

Preventing the Walking Dead

The walking dead (ON *draugar*) were a well-known pest in ancient times. Traditional psychophysiology held that part of the soul, an animating function called the *hamr*, could return to an intact body and reanimate it. The body could then rise out of the grave and go abroad causing mischief.[47] Some of the earliest runic inscriptions appear to be motivated by the desire on the runemaster's part to keep the bodies of the dead happily where they belong—in the grave where they can naturally decay, eventually freeing the soul completely.[48] Some older inscriptions include formulas such as **þrawijan haitinaR was**— "he was ordered to long (for the grave)"[KJ 61][49]—or the name of the dead will appear on a stone found inside the grave mound (meant to hold the soul name to the spot), or even perhaps the fuþark carved inside the grave chamber. This last example could mean: everything should stay in its right order, i.e., the dead man should stay in his place.

Protection from Harm

Runic inscriptions as tools for protecting individuals and places (especially sacred places) from harm are well-documented.[50] The symbolic power of the mere *presence* of runes was a forceful warning to wrongdoers in ancient times. Bracteates, the golden amulets acquired from Odinic sacred sites around 500 CE, were magical in function and were worn on the person as jewelry—apparently primarily by women.

Acquiring Love (Romantic Love)

Formulas for acquiring the love of the opposite sex were no doubt common, although they would have probably mostly been executed on perishable objects of wood or bone. These were, from a magical perspective, often coercive spells (see Skírnismál 36) or subtle workings, e.g., the weaving temple of Lund, which reads:

s k u a r a R : i k i
m a r : a f a:
(m) ạ n : mn : k r a t:
a a l l a t t i

In Old Norse: *Sigvarar-Ingimarr hafa man meingrát.* "Sigvor's Ingimar, he shall have hurtful tears." Followed by eight magical runes which communicate directly with the world of the gods.[51] The usual interpretation is that the carver/magician is in love with Ingimar's wife named Sigvor, and that the carver will take her affections away from her husband and give them to the carver—making the husband feel then as the carver does now. Here the implication is that the carving of the runes is the objective/ontological equivalent of an actual event.

Prosperity and Health

Under the general operative concept of increase, proliferation of the Good, comes a variety of magical motivations, e.g., good physical health, economic well-being (prosperity), even victory in battle (as an increase in justice). The greatest and most ancient example of this comes in the repeated use of the formulaic word *laukaz*: "leek." The leek, as a physical object in nature, is a natural sign, or true symbol, of the concept of increase[52]—it grows rapidly upward out of the dark soil from a pure white root into the light of day, shining with a green stalk and flowers in a white burst of its own light. As such it can be considered a symbolic cultural equivalent of the lotus in the East. The word *laukaz* appears repeatedly on the gold bracteates, which are categorically known to be amuletic in function.

Cursing Enemies or Evildoers

Among the most dramatic and interesting runic formulas are, of course, those which curse an enemy or evildoer. Such evildoers are sometimes personal enemies, see for example the *niðstöng* raised by Egill Skallagrímsson[53] or, more commonly, enemies of the family, clan, or tribe, who would commit sacrilege against holy traditions of the group.[54] One of the most famous of these is the curse formula found on the Björketorp and Stentoften stones (from the last half of the seventh century), which reads (in the Stentoften version):

ᚺᛁᛗᛖᛚᚨᚱᛞᛁᛦᛏᛦᚨᚠᛖᚺᛖᛏᛩᚺᛖᛗᛞᛗᚱᚺᚷᛁᛏᛩᚱᛩᛏᛩᛚ

ᚺᛗᚱᚺᛗᚾᛚᚺᛋᚺᚹᛚᛦᚱᚺᚷᚢᛈᛗᛚᚺᛗᛞᛗᛋᚺᚦᚹᛏᛒᚺᚱᛁᚾᛏᛁᚦ

H(a)id^eR rūnō ronu fel^aheka hed^era gino-r(ū)noR

heramala(u)saR ar^ageu welad(a)ud sā þat b^ariutiþ

A row of bright runes I conceal here, magically charged runes restlessly, due to "perversity," a malicious death has the one who breaks (this monument).

These objects were originally both parts of ritual ceremonial-symbolic stone arrangements. The runemaster used the inscription as a magical mode of protecting the stone settings from those in the future who might destroy the site. (Björketorp remains intact to this day.) This protection comes in the form of a curse formula, which dictates that anyone who would "break" the stone arrangement (e.g., drag off or knock over the stones for any reason) will suffer a miserable death apart from his social context. To the ancients, belonging within a strong traditional social and cultural framework was the equivalent of true freedom and security. Life apart from this, with the exception in the case of a few heroic demigods, was sure death.

Sanctifying Objects

Related to the topic just discussed is the idea that runes could be used to sanctify—set apart for holy purposes in the environment of divine protection—and object or a sphere of environment. The mere presence of runes on a stone, for example, whether in a ritual enclosure or a complex of graves, served this sanctifying function. This is most likely the long-term magical effect of many of the so-called *bauta* stones (i.e., tall single standing stones), which sometimes contain runemaster formulas, e.g., the (normalized) formula:

ᚢᛒᚨᛜᚾᛁᛏᛖ ᚺᚠ ᚱᚨᛒᚠᛝᚠᛃ ᚺᚠᛁᛏ ᛗᚲᛗᚱ ᛁᚠᚠᛃ ᚱᚾᛝᛟᚤ ᛈᚠᚱᛁᛏᚢ

ubaR hite harabanaR hait ek erilaR runoR waritu

Ubar h(a)itē, HrabanaR hait[ē]; ek erilaR rūnōR writu

(I) am called Ubar, the Raven I am called; I, the runemaster, carve the runes.

This is found on the Järsberg stone (KJ 70) from around 500–550 CE. Such stones, once having been permanently sanctified, likewise make the environment around them holy and sacrosanct.

Objectifying Inner Psychological States

The example of the Järsberg stone is also an instance of one of the most important functions of the ancient runic inscriptions—i.e., to certify and make an objective fact and reality an inner state of being possessed by the runemaster, for example. An inscription could also similarly fix the legal status of a situation or perform a number of other similar functions. Just as Óðinn, once he had received the runes (Hávamál 139), at once began to act on his knowledge by carving runes, and in so doing certified his status as a "writer"—a creator—of reality, so too does the runemaster—in imitation of his patron—carve runes objectifying his own status as a runemaster analogous to his divine patron. This act permanently transforms him, but also transforms objects so inscribed. They move permanently from a profane state into the sacred. The most obvious of these are the many *erilaz* inscriptions, of which the cliff inscription of Veblungsnes in Norway (KJ 56) is another clear example:

ᛖᚲᛁᚱᛁᛚᚨᚱᚹᛁᚹᛁᛚᚨ

ēkirilaRwiwila

ek erilaR Wīwila

I, (am) the runemaster, Wiwila (= "the sanctifier")

This particular inscription is found on a cliff face on a fjord, where it is just above the water level and visible only from the water.

Memorialization

The motivations of the last two types of inscriptions or formulas are very closely related. The majority of runestones are, on the surface, carved for purposes of memorialization of the dead, i.e., they are inscribed in memory of a named person. We know that in Germanic languages words for memory (e.g., ON *minni*) and for higher spiritual or intellectual love (e.g., MHG *minne*) are etymologically related.[55] Additionally, there is the typical memorial formula like the one found on the Heddeby stone 2 (after 934 CE), which reads (normalized):

:ᚬᛋᚠᚱᛁᚦᚱ :ᚴᛅᚱᚦᛁ . ᚴᚢᛒᛚ . ᚦᛅᚢᛋᛁ :ᛏᚢᛏᛁᛦ . ᚢᚦᛁᚾᚴᛅᚢᚱᛋ : ᚬᚠᛏ : ᛋᛁᚴᛏᚱᛁᚢᚴ :
ᚴᚢᚾᚢᚴ : ᛋᚢᚾ : ᛋᛁᚾ : ᛅᚢᚴ : ᚴᚾᚢᛒᚢ : ᚴᚢᚱᛘᛦ : ᚱᛅᛁᛋᛏ: ᚱᚢᚾᛅᛦ:

: ąsfriþr : karþi : kubl . þausi : tutiR: uþinkaurs : ąft :siktriuk :
kunuk : sun : sin : auk : kunubu : kurmR : raist : runaR:

Asfriþr gærþi kumbl þøsi, dottiR Oþinkors, æft Sigtryg kunung, sun sin ok Gnupu. GormR rest runaR.

> Asfrid, Odinkar's daughter, made this monument after (= in memory of) king Sigtryg, the son of her and Gnupa. Gorm carved the runes.

This "memorializes" not only the dead, but also the sponsor (the one who paid for the stone) and the runemaster who "signed" the inscription. We will return to the magical quality of such formulas more than once in the course of our discussions.

Immortalization

By memorializing the dead, or by inscribing the names of individuals on such stones for whatever reason, there is a motivation to *immortalize* that *name* and thus the *soul* of the individual. This motivation went from a traditional pagan rationale to an early Christian one. As we read in the *Poetic Edda* (Hávamál 76):

Deyr fé,   *deyr frœndr,*
     deyr sjálfr it sama;
enn orðstírr   *deyr aldregi,*
     hveim er sér góðan getr.

Cattle die,   kinsmen die,
     you yourself will also die,
yet "word-glory"   never dies,
     for whoever gains a reputation.

Orðs-tírr literally means "word's glory, or renown," i.e., the fame one wins recorded in words of those who survive you.

The Runic Reawakening

Our purpose here is to bring the art and practice of operative runology back to a traditional basis and rationale. Although an understanding of the historical basis of runic practice is essential to such a renewal, it must also be granted that the ancient runemasters were extremely comfortable with the use of innovative methods within their broad traditional framework. If we are to remanifest their spirit, as we have been mandated to do,[56] then this element of innovative thought and practice cannot be lost.

In the time between the demise of the traditional guild of runemasters in Scandinavia during the Middle Ages and later attempts to reawaken the tradition in the early 1600s, much of the runic magical practice was absorbed by a new hybrid Scandinavian (and especially Icelandic) magical system—which we find expressed in the famous *Galdrabók*.[57]

Sometime in the late 1300s the organized network of runemasters, aware of their venerable cultural traditions and knowledgeable of a full range of operations with runes, fell into decay. In a large part of Germania they had already been submerged, but they held out to a fairly late date in the more remote regions of Scandinavia. After this time remnants of the runic traditions were passed on piecemeal in various ways, and certain specific originally runic methods of sorcery continued for several more centuries.[58] Runic literacy continued in the Dalerna region in Sweden until the nineteenth century.[59] But this fragmenting of the tradition was really the slow process of the knowledge held by the ancient network of runemasters—the ancient rune-guild—slipping into half-slumber. The runic tradition itself is, however, immortal and eternal. The stones themselves bear witness to this reality, as they sometimes refer to the "eternal runes" and to the fact that the stones and their texts ensure the immortality of the soul of the one memorialized, just as they themselves are in fact ever-standing and steadfast through time. These outer forms are immortal—and stand waiting to be revivified and unfolded.

The reawakening of runic tradition began most dramatically with the work of the great Swedish scholar and magician, Johan Bure[60] (1568–1652). Bure not only began to reawaken our knowledge of how to read the ancient runes, but also realized the essentially magical character of the symbols. Two and a half centuries later an Austrian mystic Guido von List (1848–1919) began an even more systematic revival of the runes in connection with a renewal of the ancient Germanic religion—especially in its *esoteric* aspects.

In many ways, however, men such as Bure and von List were necessary, yet inevitably preliminary, precursors to an actual conscious reawakening of the Rune-Gild itself.

The Rune-Gild was in fact re-inaugurated during the Yuletide of 1980 in Austin, Texas by myself with the help and guidance of the All-Father and many aides and teachers here in Midgard.[61] This formal organization is still evolving, still awakening. In many ways, it remains a slumbering entity. I have taken every effort to ensure its traditional basis—going so far as to obtain a Ph.D. in Germanic and runic studies from the University of Texas at Austin, researching under one of the greatest experts in the field of ancient Germanic religion there and one of the greatest academic runologists in Germany. At the same time, every effort was maintained to keep my focus on the inner goals of the work, while synthesizing academic studies with that work at every stage. I was also greatly aided through the years by a personal association with one of the most serious initiatory schools in the world. The Rune-Gild has undergone major phases of development on a nine-year cycle, based on those recorded of the ancient cult sites at Leira and Uppsala. The Rune-Gild now stands as the major exponent of traditional runelore and operative runology in the world with qualified runemasters both in North America and in Europe. In order to be more successful and fully reawaken the glory of the ancient Rune-Gild, there is a tremendous amount of work to be done.

The Concept of *Traditional* Runelore and Rune-Work

Since the beginning of the runic revival led by the Rune-Gild, we have consistently used the word "traditional" to describe our approach to both runelore (i.e., knowledge of the mysteries) and rune-work (i.e., transformational efforts made by individuals using the rune as tools). In more recent years the study of things traditional per se has been increasingly made conspicuous through the publication of works by Julius Evola, among others.[62] Certainly the efforts of the Rune-Gild are analogous to those made by Evola et al., but not identical to them. Tradition is of decisive importance in work with the runes because it acts as an objective touchstone for the authenticity of efforts made by both individuals and groups. Such reliable guideposts are of indispensable value when navigating in an intrinsically shadowy and mysterious world. Those traveling without such guideposts usually end up over in the mud beside the road.

When I speak of tradition, I am speaking of two different, yet symbiotic, concepts. In fact, they are two sides, or aspects, of the same idea. There is the Tradition, which is a permanent set of immutable and transcendent ideas not subject to change through time, and then there is the tradition which is the historical and often imperfect process of transmitting these ideas through time, from person to person, generation to generation. The former is often differentiated, as I have done here, by capitalizing the word.

So Tradition continues to exist apart from the nature of human activity, while the quality of tradition is dependent on the excellence of human effort historically; the former is transcendent, the latter immanent.

In fact, tradition must serve Tradition in order to be authentic. The lesser tradition often seeks new and effective ways to transmit or preserve Traditional ideas. (The invention of the runic system more than two thousand years ago is an example of this.) By definition tradition involves a carrying over from one entity to another.[63] *What* is handed down is the essence of the Tradition. The lesser tradition is subject to the vicissitudes of history, the greater Tradition is not. But it must also be said that the very process of carrying on with tradition—linked to a higher source—is a part of the Tradition. The exact contents of the Tradition are not, contrary to the beliefs of some, universal. The best way to study the essence of our Tradition is to understand the essence of Indo-European ideology.

Runelore, as taught within the Rune-Gild, is Traditional. The importance of this is that it is authentic and based upon transpersonal principles and structures. The lore is not fundamentally based on the "personal revelations" of myself or anyone else. By nature this Runic Tradition is rooted in what is verifiable and objective. This allows for all individuals who seek the runes—as the essence of the mysteries—to explore an objective landscape upon which all their fellow seekers also base their explorations. Thus a community—and a guild—becomes once again possible. There is a common and Traditional metalanguage which can be referenced. Rune-work (i.e., practical, self-transformational work) in the Gild is also as Traditional as possible.

Many living in our day and time object to the very idea of tradition in any form. They fear it might stunt their "creative spirits" or otherwise spoil their fun. But our work is not in essence about having fun (a shocking revelation, perhaps, in a world of "recreational spirituality").

The reason why both Tradition and tradition are good things is that they serve as the indispensable objective guideposts to right development of the self and of the culture. They focus on what worked well in the past—and perennially—and steer us away from subjective (and solipsistic) notions, which most often prove fatal to the development of individuals and cultures. When we deeply understand Tradition, we see a spectrum of ways of being that far exceed the paradigms offered by the modernistic preachers of pseudo-diversity. Tradition offers a true diversity of being, not merely a diversity in superficial appearance. Our focus on Tradition is not an attempt to revive dead forms of practice or dead historical manifestations. We seek to reawaken what is real—eternal, great, and beautiful—slumbering within us. This is our larger mission, and this is the highest working of rune-galdor.

CHAPTER TWO

LORE OF THE FUÞARK

 In order to use the fuþark in an operative manner, the individual staves of the system must be understood. That is, they must be internalized after the subject (runer) has gained knowledge of the lore of the stave and coupled that with enough internal and external experience that a certain elevation of being takes place and a new and higher insight is gained. The lore is quite objective; however, the individual experience is necessarily subjective. This process, which is best and most fully outlined in the exercises in *The Nine Doors of Midgard* (Rûna-Raven 2004, 3rd ed.), results in a powerful synthesis of timeless transpersonal tradition and highly individualized experience and genuine understanding. Both of these factors—objective knowledge and subjective experience—must be present and highly developed for a true, living tradition to be viable and vigorous.

The individual staves (perceptible signs) are a system of symbolic qualities which serve as the traditional analysis (elemental breakdown) of the overarching concept of *Rūnō,* "mystery."

The Mystery—that which is unknown, hidden from ordinary consciousness—is the great motivator of consciousness. She drives consciousness forward to the next frontier without herself ever being exhausted and without herself ever being fully possessed by consciousness. She produces clarity and knowledge while she herself remains eternally obscure and unknown.[64] The twenty-four stave system of the Older Fuþark was the first recorded systematic codification of Mystery by the ancient Germanic peoples. For this reason, perhaps, the individual signs were referred to as "runes" (secrets, mysteries). These twenty-four are derived from a single whole, and to a great extent, the essence of higher rune-work is to recover the totality of the single mystery through conscious work with the articulated spectrum of mystery which is the **fuþark**. One of the main methods of working with the **fuþark** and coming to understand the runes is through the operative exercise of them. Development of this exercise is the aim of this book.

Operative systems are symbolic schemata through which the will of the operator (subject) is expressed in an effective and right manner such that the proper actions result in proper results. Using an operative system as their major tool, runers are able to practice a form of practical theology,[65] performative metalinguistic acts, and/or operative communication by which "things" can be done with "words." Spoken words can be powerful, written ones more powerful, and those inscribed into wood, bone, or stone more powerful still.

In order to practice the ancient art of operative runology in the traditional spirit of the original runemasters, it is necessary for us to delve into their symbolic world, make it our own in a living, breathing way, and then activate this acquired knowledge in a manner which resonates with the ideals of the ancients.

The Operative Systems

There are three traditional operative runic systems. These have been briefly introduced in a historical context in the previous chapter. The *Armanen* system is not included here because it must be considered a modern innovation or modification.[66] This is not to say that it is invalid, or that it does not continue a tradition in a new way (which all vibrant traditions are capable of), it is just that it is not in and of itself a historically traditional system. The aim of this work is to teach the runer to resonate with historically traditional systems. Likewise no special mention is made here of the Uþark system.[67] This re-encoding of the numerical values of the runes by starting with the ᚢ = 1, ᚦ = 2, etc., is in effect nothing more than a single example of possible runic code (of a kind not uncommon in late antique times) and does not in itself constitute a system radically different from the standard, historically valid system of the Older Fuþark of twenty-four runes.

The historical systems, i.e., the Older Fuþark, the Anglo-Frisian Fuþorc, and the Younger Fuþąrk, must be understood as modes of writing real languages in order to use them in advanced traditional operations.

The Older Fuþark is the most limited in this regard. Besides the older runic inscriptions themselves,[68] we have no texts suitable to act as models for new, original compositions using the language which is harmonious with the Older Fuþark. This harmony, or resonance, between language and runic system is an essential feature of radically traditional operative runology. Proto-Germanic or Primitive Norse texts should be written in older runes, Old English (or even modern English) texts in Anglo-Frisian runes, Old Norse (or even modern Icelandic) texts should be written in younger runes. By adhering to this custom, diachronic resonance[69] is possible.

To use these three runic systems properly, the runer needs to know the phonetic key to each system, i.e., which rune is written for which sound the various languages.

The Older Fuþark is quite simple. The Proto-Germanic sound system, with runes ascribed, appears:[70]

VOWELS			
	FRONT	CENTRAL	BACK
HIGH	ᛁ i		ᚢ u
MID	ᛖ e		ᛟ o
LOW		ᚨ a	

CONSONANTS			
	LABIAL	LINGUAL	VELAR
OBSTRUENTS	ᛈ p	ᛏ t	ᚲ k
	ᛒ b	ᛗ d (ð)	ᚷ g
	ᚠ f	ᚦ th	ᚺ h
NASALS	ᛗ m	ᚾ n	ᛜ ng
LIQUIDS		ᛚ l	ᚱ r
SIBILANTS		ᛋ s	ᛉ z (R)
SEMIVOWELS	ᚹ w		ᛃ j

Using this knowledge, we see that if we wanted to write the Proto-Germanic form of the name of Wōden, Wōðanaz, in older runes it would appear ᚹᛟᛞᚨᚾᚨᛉ.

The Anglo-Frisian Fuþorc is far more complex. First of all, it should be noted that Old English can be written using only the first 29 staves of the fuþorc explained in the "Old English Rune-Poem."[71] Rarer forms only found either in a few inscriptions or in manuscripts[72] extend the Anglo-Frisian Fuþorc to a total of 33 staves. Staves 30–33 may be used *optionally*, and can also be used to help write modern English in a very precise way.

Here is how to use the Anglo-Frisian Fuþorc to write Old English. No "standard" was actually established in Anglo-

Saxon England for the use of runes, as a survey of the contents of *A Concise Edition of Old English Runic Inscriptions* (Rûna-Raven, 1999) shows. Dialect and regional variations prevailed. This is a proposed current standard for the representation of "classic" West Saxon Old English:

ᚠ	= f	↑	= t
ᚢ	= u/ū	ᛒ	= b
ᚦ	= þ or ð	ᛗ	= e/ē
ᚩ	= o/ō	ᛙ	= m
ᚱ	= r	ᚱ	= l
ᚲ	= c [hard c-sound as in "cat"] or ċ [ch-sound as in cheese]	ᛥ	= ng
✕	= g [hard g-sound as in "gift"] or ġ [y-sound as in yield]	ᛞ	= d
		ᛟ	= œ
ᚹ	= w	ᚴ	= a/ā
ᚺ	= h	ᚨ	= æ/ǣ
ᚾ	= n	ᛘ	= y/ȳ
ᛁ	= i	✳	= io (rarely, if ever, used)
ᛥ	= ġ (pronounced [y], etymologically derived from PGmc. /j/)	ᛉ	= ea
ᛇ	= ï	ᚴ	= q
ᛈ	= p	ᛣ	= c [hard c-sound as in "cat" only]
ᛦ	= x	ᛥ	= st
ᛋ	= s	ᛦ	= g [hard g-sound as in "gift" only]

This system could obviously be easily adapted for use in writing modern English.

In times past, when our elder troth was fading, one of the cultural features that slowly eroded was the use of runes as a way of writing. Originally this was a system applied mainly by magicians and within the cult of Wōden. But later, and especially after Christianity and the culture of the south had made inroads into the northern world, the runestaves were increasingly brought to bear for ordinary communication. Today the runes are being revived as a magical system and as a system of initiation and self-development. For this the Older Fuþark system of twenty-four runes is most commonly used. However, as the old religion is being reawakened, it is vital that the knowledge of the runes be spread again among those who are drawn to them. Not all who learn the runes today will want to use them in the work of galdor—that is really in the realm of the Rune-Gild. But as a way to revive the intellectual traditions of our folk, knowledge of the runes and the promotion of them in religious contexts can be a great boon.

The question then arises, *what* runic system should be used for this purpose. The answer is really quite simple. As we are using English, we should use the runic system designed for and by the folk speaking that tongue. This keeps the magical tradition of the twenty-four runes separate from the everyday system which will make use of the thirty-three runes of the English manuscript tradition. Using the table presented on page 41, the reader will be able to write anything he does in modern English in runes—and have a real tradition behind him. Some slight modifications have had to be made to the Old English tradition, but they are in keeping with traditional guidelines. For those interested in the ancient and/or magical traditions, the books in the bibliography will point you in the right direction. The table is presented in the traditional fuþark order, as this is part of the intellectual heritage that the runes are intended to preserve. Every runestave has a special name which is a real word in natural language. It has symbolic meanings, which we do not have the space to go into here. We have given the New English equivalents of these names, and they should be used as the names of the "letters" when spelling something.

Shape	Phonetic Value	New Name
ᚠ	f	Fee
ᚢ	u/v	Urus (= aurochs)
ᚦ	th	Thorn
ᚩ	o	Ose (= the god = Woden) [short o]
ᚱ	r	Ride
ᚳ	c	Char (= something burnt)
ᚷ	g/j	Gibbet (= a gallows)
ᚹ	w	Wyn (= joy)
ᚻ	h	Hail
ᚾ	n	Need
ᛁ	i	Ice
ᛄ	y	Year
ᛇ	y	Yew (rarely used)
ᛈ	p	Pear
ᛉ	x	Elks
ᛋ	s	Sun
ᛏ	t	Tiw (= the god's name)
ᛒ	b	Birch
ᛖ	e	Eean (= a year-old horse)
ᛗ	m	Man
ᛚ	l	Lake
ᛝ	ng	Ing (= the god Ing/Yngvi/Frey)
ᛞ	d	Day
ᛟ	o	Odal [long o]
ᚪ	oa	Oak
ᚫ	a (æ)	Ash
ᚣ	y	Yielding
ᛠ	ea	Earth
ᛡ	eo	Yoewell (= wheel of the year)
ᛢ	q(u)	Quern (= grain mill)
ᛣ	c/k	Cup [hard c or k]
ᛥ	st	Stone
ᚸ	g	Gar (= spear) [hard g]

It will be noticed that there are more runes than there are letters in our alphabet. To write them properly, one must pay attention to, for example, whether one is writing a "g" as in "get" [ᚸ, gar], or a "g" as in "giant" [✕, gibbet]. Also, certain runestaves can serve for two Roman letters. Note: ᚦ = th, ᚻ = ch, ᚾ̊ = ng, ᛗ = st, ᛉ = ea. But all in all spelling in runes can be a matter of individual inspiration and creativity. It should never be bound by the same set of rules that apply to modern English spellings in Roman letters. If ever in doubt, use phonetics as your best guide.

The punctuation used when writing in these modern runes is as follows: All words are divided one from the other by a single dot [·], commas are a double dot [:], and periods are a triple dot [⁝].

ᚦᚢᛋ ᚠᚭᛘ ᛏᛖᚤᛏ ᚦᚱᛏ ᛅᚠᛆ ᛒᛖ ᚹᚱᛁᛏᛏᛖᛆ ᛁᛏ
ᚱᚠᛘᚠᛆ ᛚᛖᛏᛏᛖᚱᛋ ᛅᚠᛆ ᛒᛖ ᚱᛖᛁᛣᛘᚱᛗᛣ ᛁᛏ ᚱᚢᛆᛗᛋ

The Younger Fuþark is used to write Old Norse or modern Icelandic texts according to these rules, first proposed by Magnus Olsen in 1916,[73] which I used as a basis for my presentation in *Northern Magic* (Llewellyn, 1992). To write Old Norse in runes, use these rules:

Vowels

a/á	ᛆ	æn/œn	ᚴ
ö	ᛆᚿ or ᛆ	u/ú	ᚿ
ø	ᛆ or ᛆᚿ	e/é	ᛁ
jö	ᛁᚿ or ᛁᛆᚿ	y/ý	ᚿ
ei/ey	ᛆᛁ	i/í	ᛁ
æ/œ	ᛆ or ᛁ		

Consonants

b/p	ᛒ	s/z	ᛌ
k/g (c, q)	ᚼ	t/d	ᛏ
l	ᚱ	v	ᚿ
m	ᛦ	f	ᚠ

n	↑	j		
medial and initial r-	R	h		✳
final -r	⅄			

Nasals (m/n) before dentals (d/t) are generally not written, thus ᚦᚾᛏᛦ = þundr.

As a general rule, runes are not doubled, so ᛘᛁᚾᛁ = *minni*. This can be true even when the doubling would be between two different words, e.g., ᚼᚨᚾᛋᚢᚾᛦ = *hans sonr*: "his son."

One of the most difficult rules to apply involves the use of the ᚨ-rune, which stands for a/á when that sound had been followed by a nasal (m/n) in PGmc. For example, this is why ON áss (god) is written ᚬᛋ—because it is derived from PGmc *ansuz*.

All of these rules may occasionally, but not habitually, be violated for operative purposes.

Operative Uses of the Systems

Different runic systems are more suited to various operative ("magical") aims than others. Also the knowledge of the individual runer must be taken into account. If you cannot write in Old Norse, then don't try to write an original operative Old Norse text! It seems to be an obvious rule, but many modern would-be rune-magicians never seem to be honestly aware of their personal limitations. In general the *magical rule* is: Stay within systems and languages you have mastered. If you are composing an original text (requiring grammatical knowledge), stick with languages you understand. For most runers this means that the Anglo-Frisian Fuþorc should be used for most purposes. And why not? It is just as valid a traditional mytho-magical system as any other! With the rules provided, however, the runer could also be able to transliterate established words and text in Proto-Germanic or Primitive

Norse, Old English, and Old Norse into runes for *operative* purposes.

Remember that by the word "operative" I intend to convey the meaning of being able *to do things with runes.* An operative runic text energizes, focuses, directs, and refines the will of the runer in a symbolically potent manner and conceals the message in mysterious signs such that the subjective content of the runer's will is expressed in a way which is intrinsically right and proper and resonates with the ancient traditions, thus remanifesting a pattern in which the willed model of reality and the objective structure of reality are harmonized. It is too simplistic to say that we "make things happen with runes," or even that we are dealing with the "results of cause and effect." The alignment of the mysterious paradigms involved is more complex than either of those statements would imply.

Because we have no extensive reliable models and must largely rely on reconstructed forms for Proto-Germanic and Primitive Norse texts, the current use of the Older Fuþark is naturally limited to shorter texts. These texts, like those most typical of the historical Older Fuþark period, are highly formulaic, brief, and often largely nominal (i.e., restrict the use of verbs). The entire corpus of inscriptions from this period, which acts as the best instructor for the composition of original texts, is discussed in my book *Runes and Magic*. To resonate in an authentic way with the spirit of the Older Fuþark, the runer must follow the formulaic models provided by the historical tradition—just "tweaking" the formulas slightly here and there to suit one's own operative aims. For those who have studied linguistics in a formal way to the extent that they can compose texts of a longer variety, such formulas are possible in Proto-Germanic or Primitive Norse. But a word of warning here: Through the years I have known many an amateur who read a book or two and thought that it would be easy to just "wing it" when it came to creating compositions in foreign or archaic dialects. I have only known one or two who were not trained for several years in an academic setting who could actually do it. Composing runic texts and formulas, and committing them to inscriptions, cuts into the fabric of reality. Mistakes and errors can lead to unforeseen consequences.[74]

The Anglo-Frisian Fuþorc should be used to render texts in both Old English and in modern English. The latter option is a radical departure—but a natural one—in the current history of operative runology. The only slight caveat is that the modern English compositions should ideally be poetic and should avoid as much as possible Latinate words.[75] Potent passages of Old English poetry make excellent operative formulas.

The Younger Fuþąrk, of course, is to be used by those versed in Old Norse and Icelandic. This field of work is the richest one available to the current runer. There is a wide vocabulary available to express every possible thought and thus to communicate operatively on the widest possible scale while remaining entirely authentic. Also, the *Eddas* and other Old Norse pieces of literature provide thousands of formulas which can be adapted for operative purposes. Chapters 4 and 5 of this book provide numerous examples of formulas on all the systems mentioned here.

Stave-Lore

Information of an intellectual kind must first be gathered about each individual runestave; this information must be synthesized and then made a part of one's inner reality and experience through various exercises before one ever attempts to *use* runelore for operative purposes. The amount of lore available for each stave is in fact vast. Most do not realize how extensive it is. Our main and most reliable data is found in the meanings of the well-established rune-names[76] especially as expanded in the various rune-poems of the medieval as well as continuing Icelandic tradition of the *málrúnakenningar*.[77]

But there is more. Each name is, for the most part, a word in one old Germanic language or another. These words are often widely used in the old literatures. Therefore we obtain considerable amounts of nuance and information about what the rune connoted in ancient times by studying the words in context.

Occasionally, we also obtain information about the meaning of the word, or the thing the word stands for, in literatures in other languages. For example, Caesar, in *De bello Gallico* VI.28 (52 BCE), in describing some unusual animals in the territory inhabited by the Germans, writes:

> A third kind of animal is called an aurochs. In size they are somewhat smaller than elephants, with the appearance and color and shape of a bull. Their strength is great, as is their speed, they spare from attack neither man nor beast when they get sight of them. The people try to catch them in pits and kill them. This difficult task toughens the young men and keeps them fit, and those who kill the largest number show the horns in public to demonstrate what they have done, and receive great praise. No one has been able to domesticate or tame them, even when captured young. The size is greater and the shape and type of the horns is different from our oxen. [The Germans] value them greatly and mount their rims with silver and use them as drinking vessels at their feasts.[78]

Here we have an indication of what the aurochs (**ūruz*) actually meant in the context of prehistoric Germanic culture.

In my own private notebooks I have dossiers on each of the rune-names. When I come across a piece of lore relevant to that name/word/thing, I note it. I suggest all runers do the same. In contrast to what most people say, I find that traditional runelore provides a flood of information. It is the operative runologist's task to collect and *personally* synthesize it.

In general, each segment of the lore should also be subjected to a multileveled interpretive synthesis. This interpretation can never reliably exceed the capacity of the individual interpreter to carry out the task. Some can analyze on two or three levels, while others may be able to do this reliably on nine or more levels. Such levels include the physical, physiological, mythic, theological, magico-sexual, psychological, cultural, sociological, and many others.

In the study of this lore, we begin with the premise that the Older Fuþark is the basis upon which all subsequent runic systems are based, either according to the natural principle of alphabetic expansion (i.e., the Anglo-Frisian Fuþorc) or by the nonnatural principle of alphabetic contraction (i.e., the Younger Fuþąrk).

[f]

PGmc. *fehu*: "cattle, livestock";
OE *feoh*: "cattle; money, goods";
ON *fé*: "cattle sheep; property, money, gold."

The original literal meaning of Indo-European *peku-* was probably "wool-animal —> sheep," which were probably herded long before cattle. But the meaning was quickly shifted to cattle when these became the primary and most valuable herd animals in the Indo-European world. The original unit of "monetary value" was a head of cattle.

The general principle of this mystery hinges on the idea of *value*—something of worth that is easily transferred from one person to another over time and space.

In the rune-poems, two sides of this mystery are emphasized. The Old English Rune-Poem exhorts the listener, presumably a thegn or warrior, to be generous with ᚠ—giving it out broadly in order to "obtain a favorable judgment" (OE *dōmes hlēotan*). Acts of generosity on the part of secular lords bound their followers to them and at the same time constituted highly ethical behavior on their parts. They were commonly called "ring givers" for their generous distribution of wealth—generally obtained through land management, conquest, and tribute. Both Scandinavian poems refer initially to the strife caused among kinsfolk when the wealth is not distributed properly. (This is first and foremost a mythic reference to the story of the Nibelung treasure.) The *málrúnakenningar* generally corroborate these two sides of the rune. There we see such kennings for the /f/ as *firða-rögur*: "warriors' strife" as well as *peninga sjóður*: "money bag" and *vinur höfðingja*: "friend of chieftains."

In ancient Germanic culture, the idea of mobile wealth—whether in the form of livestock or valuable metal—was important economically, politically, and spiritually. Such wealth and its accumulation gave a certain quantifiable value to the possessor. Another of the kennings for /f/ is *metorð manns*: "valuation or rank of a man." Our **pecu**niary, or Plutonian, age remains quite familiar with this idea. Our times often appear to be dominated by this one facet of this particular rune. But in ancient, more honorable, and more traditional, times ᚠ bound men together in great endeavors which required steady purpose and unwavering loyalty.

In myth ᚠ is identified with the gold of the Nibelung treasure. To understand the mystery more fully, read the *Volsunga Saga* and the *Nibelungenlied* with special attention to the treasure, its genesis, transferences, and ultimate destiny.

Cosmologically, the first rune has often been associated with *fire*.[79] This is perhaps because its name alliterates with fire (OE *fȳr*), but more specifically in the Old Icelandic Rune-Poem, the kenning *flæðar viti*: "flood-tide's fire or beacon" appears. A *viti* is a signal fire or beacon, which burns on shore at the seaside to warn approaching ships—like a lighthouse. A fire in proximity to water is the cosmological key here. The world is created and sustained where fire and water meet. Fire is also necessary for the generation of gold—which is the oldest smelted metal.

Within the psychophysical world of the individual, ᚠ serves the same purpose it does in the larger body politic. It is a substance of fiery energy which triggers strong emotion (motivation) and can be easily *circulated* throughout the psychophysical system. It requires great wisdom to move and circulate this substance rightly. If it is not done correctly, it can lead to destruction as one part of the system attempts to destroy another in order to hoard the energy.

The general principle of *fehu* is that of power which can easily be transferred where it is needed in order to ensure the healthy functioning of the whole.

In operative works, it obviously would be important to the acquisition or production of wealth as well as to the distribution of vital energy to various parts of a greater system (political or individual). Two Older Fuþark inscriptions, the tanning knife of Fløksand (ca. 350) [KJ 37] and the stone of Gummarp (ca. 600) [KJ 95], use the ᚠ as a magical concept rune. Fløksand reads (normalized):

ᛚᛁᚨᚠᛚᚨᚢᚲ ᚠᚢᚠ = *lína laukaR f(ehu)*:
flax/linen, leek, wealth.

The Gummarp stone reads (normalized):

ᚺᚨᚦᚢᚹᛟᛚᚨᚠᛊᚨᛏᛖ ᛊᛏᚨᛒᚨ ᚦᚱᛁᚨ ᚠᚠᚠ
= *HaþuwolafaR sate staba þria f(ehu), f(ehu), f(ehu)*!
Hathuwolf set three staves: wealth, wealth, wealth!

From such ancient examples the best new efforts at operative runology can be gleaned.

PGmc. *ūruz:* "aurochs";
OE *ūr:* "aurochs";
ON *úr:* "drizzling rain; slag."

The original name of the rune obviously meant "aurochs," a now extinct species of Eurasian bison, *Bos taurus primigenius*. The Old Norse poems indicate the name has shifted to a homophone of the original word, although the term for aurochs still existed in Old Norse as úr. This bovine animal was the largest, fiercest, and most powerful wild beast known in ancient Europe. Its closest living relative is the Texas longhorn. As noted earlier in the quote from Caesar's text about the Germans, the hunting of this animal was a sort of rite of passage for young men. Another reason it was hunted to extinction, as Caesar also notes, was for its enormous horns, which were used as great communal drinking vessels—and most certainly in religious festivals.

In the case of the Old Norse name úr meaning drizzling rain or slag iron, we are dealing with something being *forced* out of something else, either rain out of a cloud or slag out of useful iron ore, to the general benefit of humanity.

The original general principle is one of vital *force*. This force is untamed, wild, and fierce.

Whereas the Old English Rune-Poem describes the aurochs and its characteristics directly—it is courageous (*anmōd, mōdig*), has great horns (*oferhyrned*) with which it fights, and lives out on the "moor" or wilderness—the Old Norse poems and the *málrúnakenningar* all describe "rain" or "slag."[80] Although rain is usually a good thing, as the *þurka-bann:* "ban of dryness" or the *akra-yndi:* "fields of delight," it can also be a negative phenomenon if it falls as at the wrong time, when it becomes the *hirðis hatr*: "shepherd's hate." This is a reference to the fact that in Iceland if it rained after the hay had been gathered in the field in late summer, the hay would be ruined. (Today in Iceland the hay gathered in the fields is protected with a waterproof covering, thus thwarting the ill effects of úr.)

The original significance of the aurochs in Germanic culture was as a sign of wild, untamed vitality. This contrasted with the tameness of livestock. The vital power of manhood had to be tested in the hunt against this fierce and admirable beast. Of course, the point of such hunts was that the hunter could easily be killed by the beast—this was no cowardly exercise of shooting unsuspecting animals with high-powered rifles from ambush. It was a true *test* of manly power—of virility and virtue.

Mythically this rune may be a reference to the original cosmic bovine, Auðumbla, which must have been wild because there were no humans to tame her! She shapes the original protohumanoid being, Búri, by licking him from out of a block of salt. She also nourishes the cosmic giant, Ymir (Aurgelmir), with her milk. As a shaping and nourishing force, Auðumbla is the primeval active, vital energy of the universe. This whole process, described in chapters 5–6 in the Gylfaginning in the *Prose Edda*, is connected with the phenomenon of *precipitation*. Both Ymir (Aurgelmir) and Auðumbla are created from the drops of rain which bear vital force. Curiously, the alternative name of Ymir, Aurgelmir ("mud-roarer") contains the element *aurr*: "moist earth, clay; mud," which is actually connected etymologically to the word úr: "rain."[81] *Aurr* is a mixture of the elements earth and water, which in the Eddic passage is also mixed with air and fire to form a vital, life-giving compound. The compound *hvíta-aurr*: "white-mud" is also used to describe the liquid the Norns use to nourish the cosmic tree, Yggdrasill (Völuspá 19).

The connection between bovines and cosmic vital force or energy symbolized by nourishing rains is an extremely ancient Indo-European one. Perhaps among the most archaic Indo-European myths is one in which the warrior of the gods, the hurler of thunderbolts, attacks a serpentine monster who has pent up the life-giving force of rain in the clouds (sometimes symbolized as cattle).[82] In slaying the monster, the thunderbolt releases the vital rains and renews the parched earth. This ancient link between the bovine and the rain is reflected in ᚼ, and this tradition also includes references to the storm and thunder. e.g., the idea of water forced out of clouds by Mjölnir (the hammer of Þórr) or the kenning *skjalda-fundr*: "shields' (= clouds') meeting for /u/."[83]

Within the psychophysical world of humanity, this principle is that of vital life force or energy. This is often pent up and in need of a jolt or shock to release it so that it might find its beneficial course throughout the psychosomatic system.

Ūruz is a vital, virile force of nature, wild and untamed until the will of humanity brings it under some degree of control—so that it can be made a vessel for the imbibing of this vital energy—but it can never be entirely subdued.

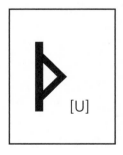

[U]

PGmc. *þurisaz:* "giant, demon";
OE *þorn:* "thorn";
ON *þurs ~ þuss*: "giant, thurs."

Conventional scholarly wisdom has it that the Old English, more "Christianized" system, replaced the overtly pre-Christian (and negative) *þurisaz* with *þorn*. For structural reasons this seems to be true, e.g., the semantic pairing of adjacent rune-names: *fehu* : *ūruz*, *þurisaz* : *ansuz*, etc. (See appendix A for a more detailed study of this idea.) However, it was also theorized by one of the greatest runologists, Wolfgang Krause, that the runes actually bore more than one name each, and that alternative names, such as *þurnuz* ("thorn") for *þurisaz*, were possibly ancient alternatives. See appendix B for an introspective list of the triadic rune-names. A *þurs* (< *þurisaz*) is a giant being connected with primeval and unconscious forces of nature, e.g., the *hrímþursar* ("rime" or "frost giants").[84] For this reason the word also came to designate a stupid or dull person (cf. Dan. *tosse*).

The : ᚦ : denotes a dangerous and aggressive force of nature, harmful to humanity and the gods. The kind of force it wields, however, is necessarily to be directed and handled by the gods, for example in the form of Þór's hammer. When turned around in this way—aggressive, unthinking force directed against the powers of chaos and nonconsciousness, the wielder, Þórr, might also be called "the good," as in the Gothic epithet *þiuþ*: "the good," which translates Greek αγαθον.[85]

Both Old Norse rune-poems emphasize that such a giant/*þurs* causes suffering to (human) women. This is because of their fierce sexual appetites as depicted in folklore—which are a symbolic expression as natural forces of their voracious hunger for the destruction of healthy, conscious, human and divine life and order. Both poems also clearly indicate another side to :x: as well. The Old Icelandic Rune-Poem stanza concludes with an identification of *þurs* as the *Varðrúnar verr*, i.e., the man/husband of a giantess named Varðrún: "secret of protection." The Old Norwegian Rune-Rhyme's second half-line reads: *kátr verðr fár af illu*: "few (*fár*) become merry as a result of evil (i.e., something bad)." This "few" could be read as a typical Germanic understatement (litotes), meaning that in fact no one at all is made happy by this, or it could be taken in another, more antinomian way—i.e., that there are those who take delight in evil.

The *málrúnakenningar* provide some insight into the *þurs*. It is called an old, ancient, proto-etin (*Fornjótur*)[86] and is specifically said to be an (initiatory) test (*þussaraun*). The link to Þórr, perhaps thought by some to be tenuous, is strengthened by the kenning *þrúðvangur*: "doughty field," which is said to be the abode of Þórr (cf. Grímnismál 4).

On the other hand, the Old English Rune-Poem is apparently an innocuous description of the thorn (bush) and its seemingly trivial dangers. Again its effects are specifically said to be evil or painful (OE *yfyl*). But here, as elsewhere in the Old English Rune-Poem, there is a difference made between a warrior (*þegn*), who might actually grasp the thorns (i.e., the active man who challenges evil), and the common, ordinary man/person (*mann*), who might find himself passively, if uncomfortably, among the thorns.

The *þursar* are the preconscious forces of brute nature which precede both the etins (ON *jötnar*) and the gods (ON *æsir*). The *þursar* are essentially and structurally opposed to the *æsir*. But this opposition is dissimilar to the one found in many dualistic systems wherein the "dark" and "light" are created coequally and thus compete on a level cosmic battlefield. The *æsir* are seen to evolve up from the *þursar*. This curiously makes the *þursar* both inferior to the æsir—because the *æsir* represent a superior form of later development—and superior to the *æsir* in that they are more basic and hence ultimately outlive the *æsir*. This is reminiscent of the much cited speculation that the cockroach will long survive the species *Homo sapiens* on this planet.

Every human, like every god, has a *þurs* lurking deep within its DNA. This thursic brain (reptilian or even deeper) is both our enemy and our friend. It is our enemy in that it works against development with its intrinsic entropic nature. But if that automatic power can be harnessed and directed toward the service of conscious plans, it can be unstoppable. The *æsir* learned to overcome and control this power for their own ends—an act which forever separated them from the thurses and made them true gods.

The thurses are the awesome forces of nature in the cosmos. Their size and lack of awareness—like gravity—make them dangerous to thinking beings (gods and humans).

In an operative context, the *þurs*-rune often figures prominently in curses or malevolent magic. One of these instances is found in the Skírnismál (stanza 36) where we read:

> *þurs ríst ek þér   ok þría stafi,*
> *   ergi ok œði   ok óþola;*
> *svá ek þat af ríst   sem ek þat á reist,*
> *   ef goraz þarfar þess.*

> I carve you a þurs-rune   and three staves,
>   wantonness and madness
>   and unbearable torment;
> I can scrape off   that which I inscribed,
>   if there be need of it.

Here Skírnir is coercing the etin-wife Gerðr to give in to his mission to bring her to his lord, Freyr, who has fallen in love with her from afar. The stanza not only shows the aggressive nature inherent in the *þurs*-rune, but also indicates that it is intensified by tripling it, that its qualities are (or can be) *ergi* (= sexual aberration, inordinate sexual desire), *œði* [< *óð*] (= madness, frenzy), and *óðoli* (= unbearable [sexual][87] torment). Additionally, we learn that the runes are activated by being carved (which we already knew) and that they can be deactivated by scraping them off.[88]

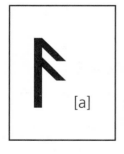

[a]

PGmc. *ansuz:* "(ancestral) sovereign god,"
OE *ōs:* "god; mouth" (< Lat. ōs) phonetic value [o];
ON *áss:* "god."

The original name of the fourth rune denotes an ancestral sovereign god. Jordanes, the Gothic historian, calls the "semi-divine" ancestors of the Gothic kings *ansis.*[89] The Old English Rune-Poem seems to indicate the meaning "mouth," borrowed from Latin *ōs*, which is pronounced in exactly the same way as the Old English word for a pagan god, *ōs* < PGmc. *ansuz*. Nevertheless the word "mouth" can be understood as a symbolic gloss for a god, especially the pagan god, Wōden.[90]

In Old Norse we learn a great deal about which god is indeed indicated with the name, i.e., Óðinn, Wōden. He is **the** áss: the original god of consciousness from whom all other gods and men—all other conscious beings—are derived, directly or indirectly. Thus, he is the ancestral god of consciousness who rules over the gods and men as a divine king.

In the Old Icelandic Rune-Poem, Óðinn is described with three kennings: *aldingautr*: "old-father"; Ásgarðs jófurr: "Asgard's chief"; and *Valhallar vísi*: "Valhalla's director." This reinforces all of the ancient ideas about *ansuz*—it is sovereign and it is the ancient progenitor (father). The Old Norwegian Rune-Rhyme and the Old English Rune-Poem, perhaps because of Christian influence, use alternate names, Old Norse óss: "mouth or outlet of a river" and the already discussed Latin *ōs*: in the Old English Rune-Poem. In both cases, however, the poet seems to allude to Odinic functions: As gods and men issue forth from Óðinn, so too do all journeys (*för*) begin out of the mouths of rivers (i.e., ship voyages) and swords come forth out of scabbards. The Old English stanza emphasizes the "mouth" as the place of origin for all speech (language), which supports wisdom, comforts the wise, and ensures the prosperity and hope of every *eorl* (earl; warrior). Again, this cleverly interprets Wōden's function as a god of consciousness, while "officially" avoiding the use of his name! For the most part the various *málrúnakenningar* indicate the later use of the word ós(s): "mouth or outlet of a river" as kennings for /o/. But two, *Valhallar vísir*: "Valhalla's director" and *manns mynd*: "a man's image" (i.e., Óðinn as the divine prototype of humanity), show clear affinity to the original name.

We are better informed about the meaning of áss than any other rune-name simply because we have so much mythology surrounding it in Old Norse literature. The Æsir are the sovereign, ruling gods of the ancient Germanic peoples. They contrast sharply with the þursar, embodied in the third rune. They also complement another group of gods, the Vanir, gods of prosperity, (re-)production, pleasure, and well-being. Those Vanir who figure in Old Norse mythology, however, are those who have been assimilated into the hierarchy of the Æsir.

The first Æsir were Óðinn-Vili-Vé (actually three hypostases of the god Óðinn). Their names mean Master of Inspiration, Strong Will, and Sacrality, respectively. They actually *evolve* from preconscious beings—thurses and etins, who are their ancestors.[91] However, the Æsir do not accept the cosmic order as they inherit it. They rebel and overthrow the old order and establish a new cosmos, refined in a rational and conscious way. They do not create the world so much as they reshape it to be more rational and beautiful. This mythology is not something best understood or *used* as a description of something that "happened" in a historically defined "past." Rather it is a myth about how consciousness—the gift of the

Æsir—must evolve, come into being and act in the world in order to do the work of the Æsir in Midgard. *This* is the actual advanced purpose of galdor and of the Runes (the articulation of symbolic sound).

Ansuz is the capacity for consciousness inherited from the gods (Æsir) through our human ancestors. This capacity gives us the power to rule as true sovereigns in Midgard, if we learn the way of the Áss, of Óðinn, which is bound to the idea of the Runes as constituting a symbolic grid-work of the elements of abstract thought and consciousness.

In operative runology, the **a**-rune may appear in a few older inscriptions as a "concept rune," or ideograph. Most conspicuously, however, it is found repeated eight times at the beginning of the B-side of the magical formula on the Lindholm bone, dated to around 500 CE.[92] Remarkably, some one thousand years later we read in the *Galdrabók*[93] a formula which begins: *Risti eg átta ása*: "I carve eight *áss*-runes . . ." This cannot be ascribed to coincidence, as both sequences occur in the context of similar formulas. Neither can there be a question of copying or the first object influencing the latter formula, since the Lindholm bone was not discovered in the bog where it had been deposited near the time it was carved until the late nineteenth century. What we have here is an example of two separate and independent attestations of a tradition of runic practice. Such examples must be studied carefully.

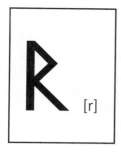

PGmc. *raiðō*: "a ride; wagon";
OE *rād*: "riding";
ON *reið*: "riding; raid; wagon."

This rune indicates both the idea of riding (on a horse) and a vehicle which might be drawn by a horse. The name is consistent throughout all three languages. In Old Norse the plural form, *reiðar*, means "a clap of thunder," as a result of Þórr driving his wagon across the sky. In Old English the word can also mean "road," especially in compound words, e.g., *brim-rād*: "brine-road" (= sea).

Raiðō is both the action and the vehicle of motion, of velocity through or over open space. This is an extremely archaic idea rooted in the primeval Indo-European cultural experience.

The rune-poems all refer to various aspects of the concept of *riding*. From their contents a clear picture emerges—this activity is comfortable and easy for the one who rides, but difficult and hard for the one who is ridden (the horse, see *ehwaz*). Clearly this concern for the horse is both a reflection of the special and ancient relationship between man ᛗ and horse ᛗ in the activity of riding ᚱ, but also an esoteric reference to the idea of the soul which in a way "rides" the body in the life process. A further indication of this comes in a reference in the Old Norwegian Rune-Rhyme to the sword (Gramr) which Reginn (re-)forged for Sigurðr. (See chapter 15 of the *Völsunga Saga*.) The sword is a repository of the soul of the warrior.[94] The *málrúnakenningar* provide only little additional information.

The original meaning of *raiðō* appears to include both the idea of riding on a horse and in a wagon hitched to a horse. In both instances, reference is made to extremely archaic Indo-European activities. The Indo-Europeans were the first to domesticate the horse. In the northern regions, people continued to ride on horseback among the steppe peoples—Scythians, Sarmatians, etc.—as well as among the Germanic peoples. Wagons were also known, but they were sometimes seen as less than manly modes of transportation. The very technology involved in all aspects of the equine culture of the ancient Indo-Europeans is of extreme importance—horse-training, fashioning of gear needed to ride or harness horses, the building of wagons with their all-important *wheels*.

Looking at the mythic references to riding, we are met with a myriad of examples. The two most obvious are Óðinn riding on Sleipnir—most perfectly depicted on the Gotland picture stones, and Þórr's riding out in his goat-drawn wagon to slay giants in the east. Notably, the rides on Sleipnir are most often seen as vertical, i.e., from Asgard to Hel or the reverse, whereas Þórr's trips are on a more horizontal plane of activity.

Within the psychophysical constitution of the human being, the riding or the traversing of time and space within the human system is effected along roadways or pathways within the psychophysical system itself. Traditional wisdom holds that such activity makes life easier for the soul, but requires *tremendous effort* on the part of the physical body, the ego, or conscious self.

Raiðō is the process of riding (movement), the vehicle in which rapid movement is made possible (energized by ᛗ), and the road- or pathway along which such movement is most efficient. This last piece of lore is of extreme importance. It indicates that development, in order to proceed most rightly, should make its way along established roads or traditional pathways. In the case of operative runology, of course, we must still clear away a great deal of debris which has obstructed our ancient tracks.

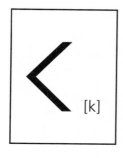

[k]

PGmc. *kēnaz:* "torch",
OE ᚳ *cēn* : "torch";
ON ᚴ *kaun:* "sore, wound" < PGmc. **kaunan:* "sore."

This rune bears two distinct names in the northern and southern traditions. This again points to the concept that all of the runes originally had three names—see appendix B. A torch is a concentrated, artificially controlled and contained fire. It is used to illuminate spaces that would otherwise be dark. A sore or wound is a form of concentrated and localized decay or destruction of the flesh—an in*flamm*ation. The latter meaning points to death wounds from battle and the flames used to destroy the warriors' bodies through cremation.

In the Old English tradition, the rune ᚳ is also made to stand for the word *cēne:* "fierce, bold, brave, warlike." This is cognate to modern English *keen.*[95]

Kēnaz is the technical[96] means through which things are transformed from one state of being to another—darkness into light, life into death, etc. Transitions are made through *kēnaz,* and such transitions are made by bold—*keen*—spirits. Such transformations are, however, rarely painless.

The Old English Rune-Poem clearly describes a torch which functions much like a modern lamp—providing light within an otherwise closed in and dark space. Typically the OERP differentiates between two classes of beings—it says that the torch is known to every living being by its fire, but that it burns with the most frequency "where the nobles rest indoors" (*þær hi æþelingas / inne restaþ*). The original could also be construed as saying: "where nobles are at rest within (themselves)," i.e., that illumination more often occurs among noble souls in a state of serenity. On the other hand, the Norse poems both refer to the name *kaun* being a sore or ulcer or even a wound received in battle (OIRP *bardaga för*), which leads to death, i.e., "makes a man pale" (ONRR *gørver mann fölvan*). The idea of a war wound is emphasized in the *málrúnakenningar* where we find *bardaga sár* ("battle-wound") and *vígsben* ("war's wound") as kennings for /k/. As those slain in battle were traditionally seen as a form of human sacrifice (to Óðinn or Týr), this association again links up with the idea of a transition from one state of being (the profane) to another (the sacred).

The cultural importance of controlled fire is tremendous—especially in northern climes where survival and visibility are often impossible without it. Some kinds of runic inscriptions, e.g., that on the stone of Eggja, were apparently carved by torchlight at night. This inscription records *Ni's sólo sott* "[The stone] is not touched by the sun" (KJ, 101). This is specifically fire in the service of humanity and human interests. It is the controlled and focused fire of the hearth, funeral pyre, and sacrificial altar.

Within the human psychophysical system, it is the manifestation of the divine fire—the light—which grows in certain people with the application of focused effort coupled with mental calm and serenity. Such inner work results in one becoming *keen*—bold, sharp-witted.

Cosmologically, the Iranians saw the element of fire as the mundane reflection of the *mind* of the Wise Lord (*Ahura Mazda*), who organically corresponds to our Óðinn.

In operative work, the power of *kēnaz* is that of causing a sign (a natural object viewed symbolically or an abstract symbol) to make a transition from the mundane world into the sacred world—and thereby sending a message to the sacred world and its inhabitants.

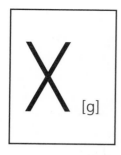

PGmc. *gēbō*: "gift.

OE *gyfu* or giefu: "gift."

This rune-*name* is not represented in the Younger Fuþark, but there are several words derived from PGmc. *gēbō* in Old Norse, among them gipt: "gift of fate, luck" and gjöf: "gift."

This rune-name is laden with profound implications in the Germanic worldview. The act of giving is the Germanic equivalent of sacrificing. In Latin *sacrificare* literally means "to make sacred (*sacer*)." In Germanic tongues the words "give" and "gift," used in a religious context, convey this meaning. Explicit in the Germanic concept of *gēbō* is the process of exchange which occurs with gift-giving. The *Poetic Edda* clearly informs us that "a gift always looks for gain" (*ey sér til gildis gjöf*) [Hávamál 145], i.e., each time a gift is given, it implies that a return gift is expected.

Gēbō is an abstract concept of the process of giving and receiving, an exchange, which acts as a way to bind together the giver and the receiver (who must in turn become a giver—if not, he is a thief). This custom binds men to one another (through gift-giving and hospitality) as well as humans to gods (in the form of sacrifice).

Although the **g**-rune is lacking in the younger rune-row, there is no shortage of references to the concept of the gift and gift-giving in Old Norse poetry. The Hávamál is especially rich in these references. The Old English Rune-Poem for : X : reads:

(gyfu) gumna byþ gleng and herenys
wraþu and wyrþscype; and wræcna gehwām
ār and ætwist, ðe byþ ōþra lēas.

(Gift) is the ornament and praise of men,
a support and honor, and to every dispossessed person
it is a benefit and means for survival
for him who is devoid of anything else.

This clearly indicates that "gift-giving" is a boon of honor to the giver and that the receiver may be a person who is poor—or *wretched*. In the process of sacred gift-giving, of course, everything is dependent upon the act being voluntary—carried out by the overt will of the giver. If the gift is pure in this way, it will not breed resentment.

As the **g**-rune was not present in the Younger Fuþark, it was later accounted for with a pointed **k**-rune (᛬ ᚴ ᛬). Among the *málrúnakenningar* the lore of the /g/ is mainly dependent upon that of the **k**-rune.

The concept of *gēbō* is the most powerful agent which binds society together. In a tribal world, such honor-bound, strictly voluntary, acts of mutual gift-giving and hospitality ensured the domestic tranquility and peacefulness of society. It is essential to recognize the mutual reciprocity of this process—a gift expects gain, and the wise donor will not give too much, nor will the wise recipient ask for too much to be given.

Also essential to the gift concept is marriage. In Old Norse *gipta* [pron. *gifta*] means "to give away in marriage." Brides were given away to the man's clan, and dowries were given to the bride's clan in order to secure the marriage. All of these gifts served to bind the respective clans together more firmly—and it was hoped—in greater *frith* ("peace").

In the mythology, the most important gift is that made by Óðinn-Vili-Vé to a wretched protohumanity when he endowed it with the spiritual (óðr, önd) as well as vital and aesthetic (*lá* and *litr*) gifts which make humanity what it is now. These gifts of consciousness are voluntarily given by the gods—but they do expect repayment for them. With these gifts comes the responsibility to use them, to develop and strengthen consciousness through effort—to wax in wisdom. In undertaking such work, humans repay the gods most directly.

Within the human psychophysiological system, certain exchanges of "energy" may take place. Each of these is a gift, a sacrifice, and a reception which requires and implies a reciprocal return gift. Only in this way is balance maintained. Cosmologically, the greatest sacrifice, the greatest act of gift-giving, is when Óðinn sacrifices himself to himself to gain the runes (universal mysteries), after which he would be able to re-create the world according to these more perfect principles.

A common Indo-European myth was that of the sacrifice of a giant (Ymir in the north, Yima in Iran) by the gods, and the subsequent formation of the cosmos out of his body parts, the clouds from his brains, the sea from his blood, the plants from his hair, etc. In Iran this came to be understood as a self-sacrifice by the deity (Ahura Mazda). The esoteric northern tradition partakes of this idea to some extent as well.

In the operative practice of rune-magic, the X-rune is used—fittingly—as a powerful binding force, binding itself with other runes. For example, on the fragmentary spear shaft of Kragehul (KJ 27), which dates from before 500 CE, we find the inscription:

ekerilaR͡asugialasmuhahaite͡gag͡ag͡aginug͡ahe
. . . lija . . . hagalawijubig

ek erilaR A(n)sugīslas muha haitē ga͡ga͡ga ginu-g͡a
he[lma-tā]lija hagla wī(h)ju bi g[aiRa]///

I, the Erulian, am called Asgisl's retainer (or son) **ga͡ga͡ga**
The magically working (sign) **g͡a**. To the helm-destroying hail I consecrate (them) by the spear . . .

The spear was ritually hurled over (or at least in the direction of the enemy army) to dedicate (give) all of those slain on the other side as a sacrifice (to the *æsir* Óðinn and/or Týr).[97]

The operative bind-runes  and  are also found on the Undley bracteate, which was unearthed in England, but probably imported from Frisia. Bracteates are categorically magical, amuletic objects. We can be sure that these bind-runes convey a magical meaning, most probably: "I give good luck, I give good luck, I give good luck—mead to the kinsman!"

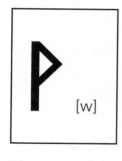

[w]

PGmc. *wunjō:* "joy,"
OE *wynn:* "delight, pleasure."
Not present in the Younger Fuþark.

The name of this rune is derived from the PGmc. root *wun-*: "love; to be satisfied." The word is also found in OHG *wunja*: "joy, desire, the best and most beautiful." In Old English the word has three levels of meaning—I: delight, pleasure (translates Latin *luxus*, *luxoria*), II: an epithet of persons or deities who bring joy, e.g., God is called *Lifes wynn* ("joy of life"), and III: the best of a class of things, the pride of its kind, e.g., *heapa wynn* ("best of troops").[98] Although the word which forms the name of this rune did not survive in Old Norse as a rune-name, it would have been **yn*, there is a suffixed form of this word—*yndi*, which does mean "satisfaction, delight."

This is the joy and delight in life—an exalted feeling of ecstasy—an existence free of woe and filled with well-being.

The Old English Rune-Poem makes the two sides of the concept behind the name clear—there is a lack of woe (*wēa*), pain (*sār*), and sorrow (*sorg*) coupled with the possession of prosperity (*blǣd*) and bliss (*blyss*)—as well as a sheltering enclosure in which to find joy. Because the name is rare in Old Norse documents, there is a shortage of information on the concept in later times—one of the lists of the *málrúnakenningar* has the kenning *ankra-yndi*: "fields' delight" for /u/. This is fascinating because the Gothic letter name *uinne* most closely matches the Gothic word *winja*: "pasture, meadow."

Culturally, *wunjō* points in the direction of the aim or *end* of human endeavors. Poetically, it comes as the end of the first *ætt* or group of eight runes. Delight is what humans aim and hope for in life. However, our ancient and traditional ancestors were well aware of the fact that such does not come easily or without hard work, effort, and often blood. The ancients lived in a world more direct and real than our own—if they did not farm or hunt, they simply starved; if they did not fight, they were killed; if they did not learn and think, their lives were empty. Real delight is the result of effort.

In the mythic and ideal world of our ancient Germanic ancestors, this concept was profound and complex. On the one hand, it was the result of harmonizing various elements on a *horizontal* plane—the society of gods or that of humans, each to its own kind. When these elements are bound together rightly, beauty and harmony result. On the other hand, the highest joy is dependent upon the attainment of the highest possible *vertical* quality. Here the individual or group is asked to aspire to a higher form of life and to rise up with inner effort to attain it. This is the secret behind Óðinn's constant trials to obtain ecstasy and with it higher knowledge. Although the Germanic mythology has often been described as pessimistic—ending as it apparently does in the destruction of the gods—the rune-row teaches us the secret lying behind the world of appearances. The mythic patterns are harshly realistic in their outlook. All that exists is subject to cyclical laws. Of course, the gods are destroyed, but they live on in new forms (Völuspá 58–63) in a renewed world of joy. The gods—and some humans—aspire to higher things and thus hurl themselves upward. The goal is joy. That this is an ancient part of Germanic ideology is shown by the fact that each of the three original *ættir* of the Older Fuþark ends in symbols of fulfillment—*wunjō* (inner joy), *sowilō* (highest visible sign of aspiration), and *ōþila* (the homeland matrix in which joy is possible).

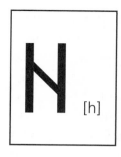

PGmc. *hagalaz:* "hail (stone)"; ᚺ
OE *hægl:* "hail"; ᚼ
ON *hagall:* "hail (special rune-name)."

All systems recognize the name and meaning of this rune as hail—hard, frozen collections of water falling from the sky. The only complication comes with the Old Norse form of the name. *Hagall* is *not* the usual word for "hail," that would be *hagl*. Therefore, *hagall* represents a special rune-name, but one which the poems clearly show is still fundamentally linked to the meteorological phenomenon of hail.

Hagalaz is a metaphor for all catastrophe. Literally this Greek word means "downturn," or "downfall." In all transformative processes such catastrophes are inevitable—and can even be made to be productive. This productivity *in potentia* is clearly recognized in the poems, which consistently identify hailstones as kernels of *grain*—i.e., seeds for further growth.

This link between hail and grain is universal in the poems. The Old English Rune-Poem says: *hægl byþ hwītust corna* (hail is the whitest of grains); the Old Norwegian Rune-Rhyme says: *hagall er kaldastr korna* (hail is the coldest of grains); and the Old Icelandic Rune-Poem says: *hagall er kaldakorn* (hail is a cold grain). Therefore *hagalaz* is a powerful, yet paradoxical, symbol of catastrophic growth. This idea of transformational productivity is further emphasized when the Old English Rune-Poem says that *weorþeþ hit tō wætere siððan* (then it becomes water)—i.e., the destructive icy stone becomes liquid nourishment.

One of the most common cultural metaphors connected with hail is the equation of projectile weapons falling on warriors with "hail." We still hear "he fell in a hail of bullets." Not only nature, but humans too, can cause catastrophe. For the most part, the phenomenon of hail was destructive to young crops and blossoms on fruit trees—as hailstorms most often occur in the springtime.

The poems and other archaic sources such as the *mál-rúnakenningar* constantly point us in a cosmological direction with respect to the esoteric meaning of *hagalaz*. The Old Norwegian Rune-Rhyme appends the statement *Kristr skóp heim-inn forna* (Christ created the world in ancient times) to ✳ —which, although obviously a Christian reference, nevertheless indicates something of the older connotations of this rune. These indications are further supported by material from the *málrúnakenningar* such as *himna-salt* (heavens' salt) and *himna malt* (heavens' malt), both of which harken back to the Norse cosmogonic myth recorded in Snorri's *Edda* (chapter 4). There we read of ice particles impregnated with salt or other vitalizing elements, such as yeast. In the same list of kennings, we find /h/ called *mari himna* (bedpost of the heavens)—a possible reference to the four posts or quarters of heaven in Norse myth. Clearly, although the primary meaning of *hagalaz* is catastrophe, it bears within itself the seed of regeneration and renewed orderly growth.

In the inner world of the runer, *hagalaz* is the sudden downturn in life—a shock delivered by the stern tester of folks—Óðinn. Such catastrophes are extraordinary gifts to those who are strong.

In ancient operative runology, ᚺ could stand for the hail of projectiles hurled or shot into your army by an enemy. We have an example of this on the Thorsberg shield-boss (KJ 21) which dates from around 200 CE. The inscription appears:

ᚺ ᚤ ᚷ ᚲ ᛁ ᚨ

and is read from right to left as *aisg(a)R h(agla)*: "seeker of hail." This means that the shield was to receive the hail of projectiles and thus protect the bearer from being hit. This indicates one of the semiotic ways in which runic inscriptions work—objects are identified with, and endowed with, the successful accomplishment of their exemplary functions.

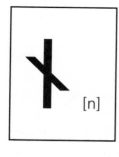

[n]

PGmc. *nauðiz*: "need, distress";
OE *nied*: "need, inevitableness; duty; compulsion; distress";
ON *nauð*: "need, distress; (pl.) fetters."

The name of this rune belongs to a rich semantic field of meaning. Throughout our sources, it carries the significance "need," i.e., a form of distress or stress—something which necessitates an effort to overcome. Etymologically, it is connected to PIE **nau-*: "to be exhausted" and refers to exhaustion preceding death. This is that point of life/death crisis which causes the soul to exert superhuman effort. There are certain things which simply *must be done* to avoid such crises. It is our duty to do these things.

The word *nauð* is inexorably linked to the idea of restriction, narrowness, and friction. This friction can, however, be turned to liberation as it is also the source of heat and even fire. *Nauð* repeatedly refers to fetters and bondage—restricted freedom. In Old Norse *nauð* can mean shackles or bondage, and in Gothic we have *naudbandi*: "fetter." Likewise, this fettering can lead to liberation, if consciousness is applied at the right time.

The application of consciousness in a timely manner is explicitly referred to in the Old English Rune-Poem which says of *nied* that it is "oppressive to the breast" but actually becomes a "help and healing" to people *gif hī his hlystaþ ǣror*—"if they listen to it early enough." The Old Norse poems allude to the restrictive, even enslaving, aspects of *nauð*. In the Old Icelandic Rune-Poem, it is called *þyjar þrá*: "the bondmaid's (i.e., the female slave's) hard struggle." The *málrúnakenningar* provide a number of insights. Under /n/ they list such characteristics as "too great a test" (*ofraun*), "loss of money," "sorrow tales," and the "dissolution of sight," i.e., the loss of sight at the end of life.

Nauðiz provides for rich cultural understanding. For the Proto-Indo-European, the greatest metaphor for unhappiness was a "narrow place"—Skt. *amhas*—restriction. By contrast, there is the great metaphor for happiness—free and rapid movement over wide-open space at great velocity with all options open. This reflects the movement of a man over the steppes in a horse-drawn chariot or on the back of a horse.

The generation of fire from friction is called the "need-fire." The oldest direct attestation for this in Germanic lore occurs in the eighth-century *Indiculus Supersitionem et Paganarium*, which is merely a list of pagan religious acts forbidden by the Church in Germany. Item fifteen reads: *De igne fricto de ligno, id est nod fyr.*[99] Note that here the original Latin uses the Germanic term *nod fyr* (need-fire)—which must have been an old sacred formula to the pagans still well-known to the church leaders. Such fires were created at certain holy times, e.g., midsummer. But the origin of the term "need-fire" must refer to the fact that such fires made from friction—creating fire where none existed previously—is something a lone traveler in the cold and dark *needs* to do in order to survive. Truly we are all lone travelers in the cold and dark.

Cosmologically, the fire which arises of the friction created by two opposing forces is an original fire. Each time it is ignited, the original first cosmic fire is symbolically reenacted, and thus a magical and vital power is released.

In essence *nauðiz* is resistance—a resistance which, if consciously understood, experienced, and *used*, can be turned into a source of energy through which the resistance itself can be overcome.

The **n**-rune occurs often in ancient operative inscriptions and formulas. In the Sigrdrífumál (stanza 7), the runic operator is enjoined to mark a *nauð*-rune on his fingernail (*merkja á nagli Nauð*). This is used to avoid betrayal and breaking of trust. More commonly the **n**-rune appears to be applied more literally as an invocation of misfortune in curse-type formulas: See, for example the famous Lindholm bone (KJ 29),[100] which has a series of three (and possibly four) **n**-runes. This formula is somewhat mirrored in the course formula in the *Galdrabók* (Spell 46),[101] which reads in part: "I write you eight áss-runes, nine *nauð*-runes, thirteen *þurs*-runes."

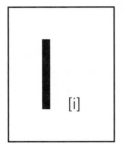

[i]

PGmc. *īsa-n* *īsaz*: "ice, frost";
OE *īs*: "ice";
ON *íss*: "ice."

The word "ice" has two variant genders, grammatically. *Īsa-n* is neuter (whence the Old English name), and *īsaz* is masculine (from which the Old Norse name is derived). This name refers to the natural phenomenon of frozen water, and its further symbolic qualities are derived from the characteristics peculiar to this phenomenon.

In the world of the early Germanic peoples, ice generally represented a dangerous phenomenon in that the freezing temperatures which cause it can also easily kill an unprotected or ill-prepared person. Additionally, the slickness or slipperiness it causes makes movement over a space more difficult for human or horse. *Īsa* itself is, however, water which has been made so cold that it is transformed from a liquid state into a solid one. Thus, what was fluid is now fixed, what flowed is now steadfast. Beyond this there is an aesthetic component: ice can appear quite beautiful to the eye.

The Old English Rune-Poem sums up all of these aspects. *Īs* is defined as "super-cold" (*oferċeald*) and immeasurably slippery (*unġemtum slidor*), but is also referred to as something which glistens clear as glass like a jewel and which is beautiful to look at (*fæġer ansȳne*). In typically paradoxical language, the rune-poems, while consistently acknowledging the dangers to transportation posed by ice, also refer to it as a *bridge* or as a "floor," i.e., a suitable surface over which to pass from one place to another. The Old Norwegian Rune-Rhyme calls ice a *brú breiða* (broad bridge), while the Old Icelandic Rune-Poem calls it the bark (i.e., cover) of a river (*árbörkr*) and the cover over the waves (*unnar þak*). So, although ice is inherently dangerous, it also enables one to pass over otherwise impassable spaces—creating a solidity allowing for transportation from one side to the other. But again, the Norse poems both insist on the dangers of this passage, with the Old Norwegian Rune-Rhyme explaining that the blind man needs to be led (*blindan þarf at læiða*) and the Old Icelandic Rune-Poem adding more ominously that ice is "a danger to men doomed to die" (*feigra manna fár*).

The material provided by the *málrúnakenningar* generally reinforces the idea of ice as a bridge or covering over water—with the added charming image of calling it a "seals' bed" (*selasæng*), i.e., an ice floe. The kennings do also add the important idea of ice being the "restriction of earth" (*jarðar-bann*). This latter idea stems back to the fundamental concept of ice being a restriction of movement, a stasis besetting dynamis—but which allows for another kind of movement, with its unavoidable dangers.

The importance of ice in the cosmology of the North is a well-known fact. This myth is most elaborately portrayed by Snorri in chapter 4 of his *Edda*. It seems unique in the history of such systems, but a closer look reveals that the original polarity is between fire and *water* and that it is only as water approaches fire that ice is formed in the watery half of the space (ON *gap*) that is filled with magical energy (ON *ginnung*). This energy is concentrated, condensed, and increased as the polar opposites approach one another to collide in the center of the forming proto-cosmos. As this occurs the ice is formed and hardened. This fire effect of expansion is reflected in the peculiar property of water that it actually *expands* when frozen. This new element of ice also provides a base of solidity for the fire so that sparks can be produced which fecundate or virtually impregnate the proto-cosmic substance with the essence of *life*. Thus ice is seen as the cosmogonic bridge element between inert matter and life.

As a side note, esoterically, an imbalance of fire is the principal agent for the "destruction" of the world in the *ragnarök* myth portrayed in the *Eddas*. This is really reinforcing the fact that the world is not being *destroyed* so much as it is being *transformed*—just as the human body is transformed into a spiritual one by the fire of the funeral pyre of heroes.

In the culture of the north, ice represents a serious, chronic challenge to humanity. In contrast to the sudden *catastrophic* effects of hail, ice speaks of the constant chill which requires inventive, "technological" remedies—warm clothing, secure structures, and fire—in order for humans to survive. As this ice requires the development of intelligence to overcome it, ice can be seen as a testing ground, and a sort of negative "instructor" in the development of consciousness.

In the mythology, of course, the element of ice, the polar opposite of which is widely seen as fire, is conspicuous. The fact that ice is seen as a dangerous—even hostile—element to consciousness is found when we encounter the so-called frost giants (ON *hrímþursar*). In the Vafþrúðnismál in the *Poetic Edda*, the cosmic giant Ymir is identified as a *hrímþurs*. Such entities can be seen as evolutionary precursors to divine, or self-, consciousness. Additionally, such entities remain in the cosmos in abundance as a challenge to those who manifest such self-consciousness. It is this challenge, as well as the solidifying and contracting aspect of ice : I : which make it a concept which suggests the development of the individual ego—the I. The ego is the chief bridge between man and the gods, but this is indeed a slippery and dangerous bridge. If the ego is seen as an end in itself, rather than a passage to a higher self, the process of development can be doomed.

In the annals of runelore, there is a medieval Latin manuscript (ninth century) called the *Isruna Tract* which outlines, among other methods, a way of encoding a runic inscription using long and short *is*-runes. Short I-runes represent the *ætt* or group of the rune, and the long ones represent its position in that group. So that ᚠ would be represented by ᛁI, ᚢ by ᛁII and so on.[102] The root of the power of this system lies in the fact that the i-rune (i.e., the straight line) is the basis, or something akin to the *prima materia*, of every runic character.

[j]

PGmc. *jēra:* "year; harvest time";
OE *ǧēr:* "year";
ON *ár:* "year; plenty, abundance, fruitfulness."

Although the word gives us our word "year," it did not originally refer to the complete solar cycle we call a year today. Rather, it referred more to a highly significant part of that cycle, namely the harvest time(s). The Indo-European word **yērō-* means a "season or year." Eventually, however, this word does become the universal Germanic term for a complete solar cycle (Ice. *ár*, Swed. *år*, Eng. *year*, Ger. *Jahr*, etc.) measured from one significant point to another. Sometimes this point is Midwinter (Yule-tide); at other times, e.g., in the Viking Age, it was the end of harvest time (Winter Nights, ON *vetrnætr*). This latter period was also viewed as the beginning of a new annual cycle, or new year. In either case, it can be seen that the most ancient Germanic peoples counted their "years" by *winters*, just as they counted their "days" by *nights*. The new day began at sundown, not at sunrise, the new year either in fall or winter. The Germanic new year being in the depth of winter has now been universalized throughout most of the world.

The true significance of *jēra* is twofold: 1) it is the ending and beginning of a cycle, and 2) it is the time in which what has been sown is reaped. The older shape of this runestave, one of the number of staves clearly not based on a Roman model, is an icon of the dividing point in a cycle: ᛃ.

All of the rune-poems point to the idea of *harvest* as a benefit to human beings *universally*. Both Norse poems repeat the phrase *ár er gumna góði:* "harvest is the profit of men." The English poem says: *ġēr byþ gumena hiht:* "harvest is the hope of men," and further emphasizes that it is good for both rich and poor (*beornas and þearfas*) alike. This theme is generally repeated throughout the lists of *málrúnakenningar* under the letter /a/. But in a few of the *kerfi* among these, there is also reference to the benefit of birds (*fugla-fögnuðr:* "birds' good-cheer" and *fugla-söngur:* "birds' song," i.e., something that makes them sing). There is also a more enigmatic kenning—*Siglufákur á ferð:* "a mast-horse [= ship] on a journey." This could be an archaic reference to the use of boats in harvest processions, to the "fruits" borne of Viking raids, or more ominously to the idea that the dead are transported from this world the next in ships. Similarly, if the birds mentioned are ravens or eagles, the "harvest" could be the corpses of warriors on the battlefield. The harvest is the completion of a cycle, only possible once the crop has reached a ripened state—hence the kenning *algróinn akr* in the Old Icelandic Rune-Poem.

The ancient Germanic peoples were by necessity very much aware of cycle in nature—in the plant and animal kingdoms as linked to meteorological and astronomical phenomena—as knowledge of them was needed for their very survival. In order to take proper advantage of the benefits of these cycles, certain actions had to be performed at the right times. The most critical times were at the beginning and ending of these cycles—sowing and reaping. The midpoints between these critical activities, i.e., Midsummer and Yule, are times of celebration and rest. *Jēra* is also closely identified with summer, hence the kenning *gott sumar*, "good summer" in the OIRP.

These cycles are also deeply understood within the mythic conceptual world of the ancients; the concept of *ragnarök*, "judgment or discourse of the gods [= divine advisors]," is as much about the beginning and midpoint of the cosmic cycle as it is about the end. *Jēra* is a mythic sign of the cycle of all events and a guide to how these cycles are used by the gods—especially Óðinn—and how they *can* be used by men. *Ragnarök*, properly and completely understood, describes how all things came into being, live and flourish, and then eventually pass away to allow for a fresh regeneration. This dynamic model is the Germanic ideal—change and flux in an ordered framework leading to a continual eternity of recurring springs. But in order for there to be a spring, there must be a fall—a harvest. In the Odinic mythology of Valhöll, we see that the god engenders, cultivates, and develops heroes in Midgard—only to have them cut down in their prime like so much wheat. He does this, we learn from skaldic poetry, in order to swell the ranks of Valhöll with the finest heroes needed in the final battle of the cosmic cycle. For it is those who take part in this final battle who will live in a truly eternal manner.

Jēra describes a mechanism in the psychophysiological makeup of man—or god—by which luck (ON *hamingja* or *gæfa*, or *heill*, etc.) is produced and engendered. Luck is tantamount to a concrete power stored in the essence of the individual. Its production is dependent upon the performance of right deeds (i.e., thoughts, words, and actions) at the right times. The process outlined by *jēra* goes on regardless of an individual's state of consciousness or knowledge. Luck is then produced or destroyed haphazardly. The runer learns the laws of the Unknown and applies them in a manner calculated to produce as much positive effect as possible. All actions resonate with their own quality and quantity. Thus what we call the "future" and the events occurring there are the resonant results of today's words, thoughts, and actions. If you plant an acorn, an oak tree will grow.

The early historical record of runic inscriptions contains several references to the operative power of *jēra*—used as an ideographical rune meant to infuse the inscription with the meaning of the rune as an isolated idea on occasion. Some of those examples tell us little about the overall intent of the runer who carved or composed the inscription. One operative inscription which offers more about the context is the stone of Stentoften (carved around 650 CE). It reads in part (in normalized runes):

ᚺᛁᚾᚢᚠᚷᛗᛋᛏᚢᛗᛃ ᚺᛁᚾᚢᚠᛒᛉᛉᛞᛗᛃᚾᚨᚦᚢᛉᛚᚠᚠᛃᚷᚨᚠ⟨

To the new farmers, to the new foreigners,
Haþuwolf gave good harvest.

The word *jēra* is given only as an ideographic rune ⟨. By this method the runemaster emphasizes the concept as a higher encoded principle and thus activates it magically.

The *j(ēra)* is marked by being indicated only as an ideographic rune. It is used here parallel to the magical word-formula *auja*: "good fortune." This alignment shows that rune-names themselves were considered by the ancient runemasters to be the equivalent of magical word-formulas.

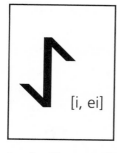

[i, ei]

PGmc. *eihwaz*: "yew (tree),"

OE *eoh*: "yew (tree),"

ON *Ýr* (ᛦ): "yew (tree); bow made of yew wood."

In the Younger Fuþark the *ýr* is moved to the end of the row, which is authentic to its almost exclusive use as a final [-R, -r] grammatical marker. (It thus assumes the phonetic role of the older ᛉ-*elhaz*-rune [-R].) Later still, the Norse rune takes on the value of its initial sound [y-].

The name of this rune clearly denotes the yew (*Taxus baccata*). Etymologically, the word is derived from an Indo-European term **ei-*, meaning "reddish." This is due to the reddish color of the yew wood, or perhaps due to its distinctive red berries, which contain a strong neurotoxin. Yew wood is particularly well-suited to making bows to project arrows, and for this reason the word "yew" came to be colloquially synonymous with "bow."

Yews were planted in English churchyards, i.e., graveyards, both as symbols of eternal life and as an ongoing and protected source for the production of bows for military purposes. It is likely that such yews were originally part of pagan sanctuaries, and that the association between yews and places of worship was so strong in people's minds that the tradition was carried forward.

A kenning for fire is *ýs angr*: "yew's bale."

The fundamental principle behind the mystery (rune) of the yew is that of vertical (i.e., spiritual) polarity. The yew connects and synthesizes vertical polarities—up : down, life : death. The yew is the central *axis* of the older runic system, and the outermost *limit* of the younger system.

Poetic records provide different viewpoints on the meaning of the yew. The Old English Rune-Poem emphasizes its role as a tree with firmness and steadfastness as its dominant characteristics. It is rooted to the earth, which gives it its special abilities to serve flexible and various esoteric functions. The yew is full of ambiguities and paradoxes, and this is reflected in its poetic uses. The Old English Rune-Poem says the yew is "rough on the outside," a veiled reference to the opposite quality of its interior—being smooth, hard, and flexible. The final word the Saxon poet has to say about *eoh* is that it is a *wyn on ēþle*—"a joy on the estate." Here we are presented with a triad of runes as both ᛈ *wyn(n)* and ᛟ *ēþel* are rune-names as well: ᛇ = ᛈ/ᛟ. The "runic equation" or complex formula is decoded as follows: ᛇ provides the necessary element (*vertical* connection) for there to be happiness (*wynn*) not only in the world of men and nature (see *ōþila*) now (synchronically), but over time (diachronically) as well. As a symbol in nature of steadfastness, it is also a reflection of the more permanent and complete world *above* (i.e., Ásgarðr).

The *málrúnakenningar* provide us with little new information.

In the world of northern mythology, we find that the cosmic realm called *Ý-dalir* (yew-dales) is said to be the home of the god Ullr. He is the bow god, and is also symbolically linked to the yew as the material for fashioning bows. Curiously, this god is only worshipped in a specific area of Scandinavia. Place-names indicating where his cult sites were in ancient times show this to be central Scandinavia. In precisely these areas we also find that place-names indicating the worship of Týr are generally missing. Thus the names are in "mutual distribution." This would indicate that there is a certain functional equivalency between Ullr and Týr. On the surface, they appear dissimilar, but a key can be found in the runes they represent: Ullr = ᛇ (ᛉ) and Týr = ᛏ. Both are important as vertical axes which both separate and unite heaven and earth.

The lore of the yew tree, the iconic appearance of the rune :ᛇ:, as well as more abstract mythic references, all point in the direction of this being the embodiment of the idea of a unity of polar opposites or extremes along a vertical axis.

In the study of the doctrine of runic dyads (see appendix A), the :ᛇ: is logically and formally paired with :ᛈ: for reasons that will be clear in the discussion of that rune. However, :ᛇ: forms a special and unique secondary dyad with :ᛃ:. There is in fact a whole system of secondary dyads, which give rise to the so-called Uþark code. The center of the runic system lies between :ᛃ: and :ᛇ:—the cycle and the axis or ring and pole of the world.

In the realm of practical magic, the yew seems to have held a special place in ancient times.[103] Runic inscriptions are found in yew wood. One of the most interesting is the mysterious box of yew wood from Garbølle in Denmark (ca. 400 CE). The side of the small box with a sliding top is inscribed with the runes:

ᚺᚨᚷᛁᚱᚨᛞᚨᛉᛁᛏᚨᚹᛁᛞᛖ

hagiradaRitawide

HagiradaR ī tawidē

Hagirad made (the runes) in (the box)

More telling than runes being carved in yew wood—which seems to be an ideal carving substance both practically and mythically—is when *yew* is actually referred to in the content of the inscription. An example of this is found on the eighth-century Frisian yew wand of Westeremden (B), which one interpreter translated:

Amluþ took up position against Opham.
The surf submitted to the yews,
the surf will submit to the yew.

If this interpretation is correct, we would have an example of the seas being calmed (for ease of a military operation) by the power of the yew force.

PGmc. *perþrō:* "pear(-tree),"
OE *peorð:* ["game piece"?].
There is no Old Norse cognate for this name or word.

The name of this rune is problematic for most scholars. All we know about it is contained in the various lists of rune-names, the Gothic letter name *pertra*, and the Old English Rune-Poem which generally describes some object which is always *plega and hlehter*—"sport and laughter"—to warriors in the hall. A key to its meaning is contained in the idea of runic dyads. We see that ᛈ is paired with ᛇ Clearly, ᛇ refers to the yew tree, which makes it more likely that ᛈ also refers to a tree. The name remains problematic. Insight leads us in the direction of identifying it as a fruit-bearing deciduous tree to contrast with the coniferous yew.

Tacitus reports how much the Germanic warriors liked to "gamble" in *Germania*, chapter 24. Gambling was a form of a "test of luck" one man against another—as were all contests or conflicts in the ancient Germanic world—military or legal. This led scholars such as Karl Schneider to conclude that the **p**-rune has something to do with this concept of testing of fate or luck in a sort of divinatory game played in the hall of the chieftain.

The general principle of *perþrō* is that of *change*. With this change come good things or bad. What is certain is that there will be a shift or flux. The Germanic mind is strangely comfortable with this idea. It sobers and prepares the mind in good times and gives hope in bad times.

As mentioned above, our only concrete evidence for the meaning of the **p**-rune is contained in the Old English Rune-Poem which reads:

(Peorð) byþ symble   plega and hlehter
*   wlancum [on middum]*
*   þar wigan sittaþ*
on bēorsele   blīþe ætsomne.

Peorð is always   sport and laughter
     to the proud ones in the middle
          where warriors sit
in the beer-hall   happily together.

The ancients loved to test their luck and prove themselves in such games. Schneider speculated that the shape of the rune was a reference to a cup used to shake "dice" for such games of chance.[104]

The *málrúnakenningar* strangely seem to have preserved some of the essential lore surrounding this ancient rune. We see that the /p/ is referred to as "burning pain inflicted by the norns" (I:p), or an "easily upset life" (VI:p), or even in the ominous "anointing arrival," which may be a reference to the last rites before death (extreme unction). But true to the apparent nature of *perþrō*, we also see kennings of a very positive kind, e.g., "tried and true relief" (II:p), "ointment medicine" (III:p), "good life" (IV:p), and "healing of injuries" (VIII:p). From all of this it seems that the lore surrounding the magical letter /p/ remained informed by the ancient ideas connected to *perþrō*.

Of the things we know about the p-rune, the best documented ones connect it to games of chance or strategy among noble folk. We are reminded that in the *Völsunga Saga* Reginn, the foster father of Sigurðr, teaches the young hero three things: languages, *tafl*, and runes. "Languages" probably meant something of the differences between and among the Germanic dialects, and "runes" probably indicated mere writing in runes. (Only later and by his own *valkyrja*, Sigrdrífa, would Sigurðr be initiated into the runic mysteries.) But *tafl* was a board game of strategic importance widely played in the north and northwestern parts of Europe. All games, whether of chance or skill and strategy, teach us about the consequences of actions—and often unforeseen outcomes and apparent "strokes of fate."

Germanic myth often seems to show Óðinn as a supreme cosmic strategist. He plies his wits against the forces of wyrd and entropy in the service of the development of divine consciousness. In these games Óðinn demonstrates his mastery in that he is not averse to using the very forces he appears to strive against in order to attain his goals.

Within the cosmos, as well as the psychophysical realm of the individual, the forces of disorder and unforeseen results of actions undertaken in the past are of tremendous importance. The maintenance of a stable balance within the dynamic flux of change and tumult is the Germanic ideal. This is an ideal that is supremely difficult to master, as the forces of oppressive entropy and disorganization are always quantitatively stronger than those refined and delicately balanced qualities of consciousness.

The *perþrō* is a sign of change (a deciduous tree) which appears to die and be resurrected to life on a cyclical basis. It is flux and dynamic balance.

Operatively, the p-rune and its symbols are rarely seen outside the context of complete fuþarks. The Proto-Germanic language used the sound [p] only in a few words—many other examples of it are in terms borrowed out of Latin. Even phonetically, it holds a unique position. In operative rune-magic, the concept of *perþrō* is key in that it is the dynamic force of flux in the world which the runer seeks to guide or control, yet it is this very force which is necessary to the operator of runes to be able to impress his will upon the fabric of this dynamic field.

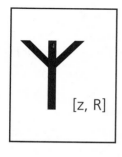

[z, R]

PGmc. *elhaz:* "elk";
OE *eolhsecg:* "elk-sedge" [x].

The phonetic role of this rune was taken over in the early phase of the Younger Fuþark by the ýr-rune. (See the discussion under the *eihwaz* rune.) The ON word derived from *elhaz* is *elgr*: "elk." *Elhaz* is also obviously the etymological source of the English cognate, "elk."

There is some disagreement among runologists as to the actual form and meaning of the name of this rune. Some reconstructed the name as *algiz*: "protection," or this form is also sometimes also translated as "elk." These controversies are, however, easily resolved and redirected once it is understood that the runes originally had more than one name. (See appendix B.) The Old English rune-name in the poem is a compound of *eolh* and *secg*, the phonetic value in Old English is given as [x], a sound naturally made when a [k/h] is followed by an [s]. In the lists of rune-names found in *runica manuscripta*,[105] the name appears in a variety of forms, e.g., *eolhx*, *iolx*, *ilx*, *ilcs*, or *ilix*.

Clearly, the oldest common form of the name and the iconic code for the concept was the elk—Latin *alces*. The principle at work here is a manifestation of the "highest" of the earth. The connection with exalted divine power infuses the individual person or thing with a force which provides true life, protection, and knowledge.

We only have one poetic stanza relevant to this rune, that found in the Old English Rune-Poem. Unfortunately, it is a commentary on the secondary designation of elk's sedge—a water plant with sharp leaves which may cut anyone who tries to grasp them. This all alludes to its protective function. The *mál-rúnakenningar* are of little help as well. The Anglo-Saxon lore linking this rune with the phonetic value [x], and its replacement by the ᛉ-rune in Scandinavia and then the shift in value of the ᛉ-rune to [y], and the old [R] being eventually replaced by /r/, all conspire to leave us with little objective information about *elhaz* from the most common sources.

Fortunately, lore surrounding the elk and some comparative Indo-European evidence provide us with what we need.

Elhaz covers a variety of horned "deer"-like animals. Our modern English word "deer" is really an ancient designation of an animal of *any* kind. For this was *the* animal, the beast, par excellence. The full grown male was called a stag, while another name was "hart" or "hind." This kind of animal was widely hunted, of course, as it is today. The Old Norwegian Rune-Rhyme, in the second line of the stanza referring to the **u**-rune, says: *opt helper hreinn á hjarni* ("the [rein-]deer often runs on hard-frozen snow"), apparently a reference to how they were typically hunted—being run or chased out onto frozen surfaces. One Old Norse kenning for ice (*íss*) is "elk-gallows,"[106] i.e., a place where elk are killed. But the deer was also one of the first animals domesticated by the early Indo-Europeans, perhaps even before the horse. This archaic domestication, and sanctification, is reflected in the Scythian custom of "disguising" their horses as deer—fitting them with artificial antlers—for ritual purposes.

Germanic myth and legend are rich in images of the elk or stag. The greatest and highest of all ancient Germanic heroes Sigurðr/Siegfried is continually linked to this kind of animal. In the *Þiðreks saga* (chapter 162), Sigurðr is fostered and suckled by hinds as an infant. When Sigurðr kills the serpent Fáfnir, he tries to disguise his name at first by calling himself the *göfugt dýr* (noble beast), which is a well-attested kenning for a stag (Fáfnismál 2). Finally, when Sigurðr awakens his *valkýrja*, Sigrdrífa, he does so after ascending the mountain atop which she lies in a magical trance. This mountain is called *Hindarfjell* (Hind-Mountain). So at birth, during central heroic act (dragon-slaying), and at his awakening to his higher self and into the runes, Sigurðr is linked to the ᛉ. It should not go unnoticed that these stages all reflect Dumézilian trifunctionality: I birth (fertility); II warrior-act (dragon-slaying), and III initiation into wisdom.

This linkage of the stag to higher pursuits or the divine realm appears to be an Indo-European trait. The Scythians saw the deer as having significance to heavenly transformation of their horses, and in the Old Irish heroic cycle of Finn mac Cumhaill, the stag is seen leading men off into the deep woods for otherworldly encounters.

Cosmologically, the most intriguing example of the symbolism of harts involves the four cosmic stags stationed at the four quarters of heaven (*Edda*, chapter 16). There names are Dáinn, Dvalinn, Duneyr, and Duraþror. They are said to gnaw the leaves of the cosmic tree, Yggdrasill. Two of their names are also known to be names of dwarves (Dáinn and Dvalinn). This suggests that there is a close relationship with the four dwarves said to be stationed at the quarters of heaven: Norðri, Austri, Suðri, and Vestri (*Edda*, chapter 8), whose "names" appear to be contrived.

Stags seem to have a variety of functions—they guard the quarters, lead and nurture heroes, and have a destructive effect on the cosmic structure at its outer edges.

In the psychophysical makeup of the individual, the energy of *elhaz* is that which conducts vital, organic force in an upward, vertical direction. It is the urge to attain the highest, welling up from the earth, upward to the heavens.

In the ancient record of runic inscriptions, there are some interesting uses of the symbolism of the deer or elk. The Fællesje tanning knife made of antler from around 500 CE bears the inscription ᚹᛁᛏᚱᛟ *witring*—"writing; proclamation." The Caistor-by-Norwich (fifth century) has the inscription *raïhan* on a deer bone—which may designate the runemaster as "the colorer," or "the scratcher."[107] Most intriguing of all, however, is the wooden footstool of Wremden, dated precisely to 421 CE. Its inscription reads:

scamella **alguskaþi**

This is best interpreted as a Latin word for footstool plus the Germanic compound *algu-skaþi*: "elk-harmer." The *scamella* is the kind of footstool used by kings as they sat on their thrones so that their feet did not rest of the same floor as other people. And the artistic work on this object depicts a scene of hunting an elk—a well-known, prestigious royal activity.

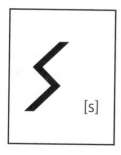

[s]

PGmc. *sowilō:* "sun"
OE *sigel* [seeyell]: "sun";
ON *sól:* "sun."

There is unanimity in the tradition concerning the meaning of this stave—the sun. The name is, however, different from our modern English word *sun*, which is derived from another Old English word *sunne*, also meaning "sun." In Old Norse we also see these two separate words, *sól* and *sunna*, for the sun. The word *sowilō* in its derived forms shows a propensity to being identified as an "eye," e.g., OE *heafdes segel:* "head's sun" [= eye], and in Old Irish *súil* means "eye." Early English folk etymology probably made a connection between *sigel:* "sun" and *sige:* "victory."

The principle of *sowilō* is that of a transcendent goal of the hero, which is the highest of life and which provides for life, energy, and well-being. *Sowilō* is itself unchanging, but ever moving.

All of the rune-poem stanzas clearly refer to the sun. The Old English Rune-Poem brings together the ideas of a sea journey and the sun. This invokes one of the most ancient and enduring images of Germanic prehistory, as exemplified in the Bronze Age rock carvings—that of a boat or ship in which the sun rides, or over which it hovers:

The OERP stanza focuses ultimately on the idea of the *purpose* of the journey and the role of the ship and sun: the trip is to reach the other shore, and the ship is the vehicle of transportation while the sun provides guidance and *hope*. The environment in which this journey takes place is turbulent and often chaotic. Interestingly, the Old Irish word, *súil*, mentioned above, means both "eye" and "hope." The Norse poems tell us that the sun is the light of the land and the "sorrow" (destroyer) of *ice*. (When one rune-name appears in a stanza which describes another, obviously special attention is required.) It is also characterized as a shield and a wheel. It has protective functions, and it is mobile and provides for motion. The sun was historically an object of veneration, as reflected in the Old Norse Rune-Rhyme which says of *sól—lúti ek helgum dómi*, "I bow to the judgment of the sacred." This is acknowledgment of the sun as a symbol of the idea of a "higher power" in the universe.

The *málrúnakenningar* provide some interesting nuances. One kenning given is that of praise or fame, which is earned by one manifesting one's highest goals and principles. Another intimates that the sun is available to all men along with its power and light. The kenning *lyða ljós* uses a word for "people" which means "all the people in common." The kennings also return to archaic images of the wheel and the eye with the formulas *Ymis-auga*, "the eye of the giant Ymir," and *hjóla-haukur*, "wheel-hawk."

In the north, the sun is understood as a warming, nurturing, and life-giving force. Traditionally, it is seen as feminine—and expresses the consistent power of the feminine to establish and maintain good healthy order in a society. The sun and the moon along with the stars provide order to human life and are the markers of the orderly passage of time.

The sun, especially the rising sun of the morning, was revered by the ancient northmen. One of the verses used to greet the morning sun probably survives in Sigrdrífumál (stanza 3):

Heill dagr, heilir dags synir,
  heil nótt ok nipt!
óreiðum augum   litið okkur þinig,
  ok gefit sitjandum sigr!

Hail day, hail the sons of day,
  hail the night and her daughter!
with friendly eyes look upon us two,
  and give those sitting here victory!

That such greetings are not mere fantasy is demonstrated by an
old Icelandic custom of children who would get up out of bed
in the morning, rush out, and say a prayer or recite a verse to
the sun. Then, and only then, could the child bid anyone else a
"*goðan daginn*" (good day). These sun-greeters are thought to
be "fetching a good day."[108]

In mythology, various goddesses are linked to the sun. Sunna
is the name used for the deified sun herself in Icelandic. But it
would appear that Freyja was also closely related to the sun—
in Germany when the sun is hot, people say: "*Die gelbe Sau
brennt*"—"the yellow sow is burning" in a clear reference to the
porcine associations of the Vanir. Also, a kenning for amber is
sólartár, "sun's tears"—a reference to the tears of Freyja turning
to amber as she weeps for the lost Óðr.

Generally, however, the heavenly bodies are seen as important manifestations of unseen patterns of order. In the case of
the sun, by her movement she orders the day and night, the summer and winter. In the cosmogony, it is said that the sun at first
did not know what course to take—until Óðinn reconfigured
creation and established a good and rational order (Völuspá 5).
Conversely, in the eschatology, the sun and other heavenly bodies are said to be subject to chaotic forces:

Sól tér sortna,　　　*sígr fold í mar,*
hverfa af himni　　　*heiðar stjörnar.*

The sun turned dark,　the earth sank into the sea,
from the heavens fall　the bright stars. (Völuspá 57)

Within the human psychophysiological (soul-body) complex, *sowilō* is the indwelling transcendent goal or focus of individual development. Without this internal sun, there is no suprarational motivation for extraordinary strivings of the human spirit.

Operatively, *sowilō* presents many interesting aspects. It is paradoxical in many respects: it constitutes an unchanging transcendental ideal, yet is the most variegated among runestaves as far as the history of its form is concerned. The s-rune may appear in may shapes:

The sun itself can have an effect on the operation of rune-magic, as we learn from the inscription on the stone of Eggja (ca. 700), where we read:

ᚺᛁᛋᛋᛟᛚᚢᛋᛟᛏ

ni's sólu sott

(The stone) is not touched by the sun.

As this is a curse stone and a part of a burial chamber, it is obvious that such formulas were to be executed in darkness, not illuminated by the natural light of the sun.

In northern magic, we often see examples of how the light of the sun or moon will have either beneficial or detrimental influence on the success of the working.

On an iconographical level, two s-runes can be seen as being combined in a bind-rune to form a solar wheel:

and this is often seen incorporated into the design of the Christian cross on Swedish runestones in this form.

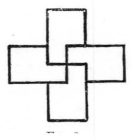

Note that here the cross is the equilateral one of the militant orders (e.g., Templars) rather than the more usual Latin cross: ☩. In Sweden this icon is at the center of hundreds of runic inscriptions which stand in the open air under the natural sun.

[t]

PGmc. *teiwaz:* "the god Týr";
ON *Týr:* "the god Týr";
OE *tir:* "glory, honor."

Perhaps because the original name of this rune was that of the pagan god of the sky and of justice, Teiwaz, the name was altered in the Anglo-Saxon tradition. The Old English word *tīr* sounds much like the Scandinavian name of the god, but means "glory" or "honor." The OE form of the name should perhaps be Tīw, the Old English form of the god's name giving English speakers the weekday *Tīwes-dæġ* > Tuesday. Semantically, however, the Old English term does not seem to diverge that greatly from the mythic association of the god. The PGmc. *teiwaz* is derived from PIE *daius* which is also the direct root of the divine names Jupiter (Latin) and Zeus (Greek). Teiwaz is the archaic sky god and the enduring god of law and justice.

The central principle of *teiwaz* is that of a transcendental set of laws in the cosmos which encourage good and combat evil. These laws exist above and beyond the natural world, but nevertheless infuse it with an omnipresent goodness.

Both of the Norse poems clearly refer to the pagan god Týr (Tīw). These poems both also point directly to the most important myth surrounding the god Týr: his sacrifice of his hand to the Fenris-wolf in order to preserve peace and tranquility among the Æsir. The poems refer to Týr as a "one-handed god," and the Old Icelandic Rune-Poem adds that Týr is to be defined as the "leftovers of the wolf"—i.e., what remains after the wolf has consumed his hand.

This myth is worth retelling briefly, so that we can understand the essence of the Tyric principle.

Loki ("Terminator") and his mistress Angrboða ("Boder-of-Sorrow") had three children together: Jörmungandr (Midgard's Serpent), Hel (Death), and Fenrir (Wolf). Jörmungandr was cast out into the great ocean around the world where it lies biting its own tail, Hel was given dominion over the nether regions, but Fenrir was at first taken in by the Æsir and raised by them. Týr was the only god who could feed this ever more aggressive beast. The gods came to fear the increasing power of the Fenris Wolf—and so they conspired to bind him. They tried three forms of fetter. The first Lœðing (trickery) and the second Drómi (restricter) were both broken by Fenrir. They then had the dwarves make a third fetter called Gelgja (pole). It was composed of six ingredients—each a metaphor for "nothingness" or "nonexistence." The Wolf was suspicious of this fetter, and demanded that Týr place a hand in his jaws as a pledge of good faith before submitting to it. When the fetter held, the Wolf bit off Týr's hand—and thus he gained his names "the one-handed god" and the "leftovers of the wolf." Some might suspect this myth to be a recent Icelandic literary invention—a "charge" often leveled at the antiquity of Eddic lore. Such statements are usually made by those who wish to denigrate the tradition for "political" or religious reasons. In fact, this, like so much else in the *Edda*, is extremely archaic. Some *700 years* before Snorri penned his manuscript, we can find bracteates with clear images of Týr, with his characteristic weapon, the sword, and holding his hand in the jaws of the Wolf.

Týr's power is in his moral authority, his willingness to suffer for the benefit of the community of conscious beings—gods and men alike. It is this power which makes him what the OIRP refers to as the "protector of temples" (*hofa hilmir*).

The Old English Rune-Poem does not use the OE form of the god's name (Tīw) as the rune-name, but rather substitutes a word that sounds like the Norse name, *tīr* [teer], meaning "glory" and "honor." However, the poem clearly states that *tīr* is some sort of "sign" (OE *tācn*) and describes what must be a star or constellation of stars in the night sky above the clouds—probably the polestar—and adds pointedly that it never fails (*næfre swīceþ*). Thus the principles of Týr are transferred to a physical phenomenon which reflects his essence—transcendence, polarity, and steady reliability.

In the *málrúnakenningar*, several kennings refer to the myth of the Wolf, one intriguing one also giving a possible clue to the star system referred to in the OERP—*banda-vagn*, which literally translated means "fetters'-wagon or vehicle."

But the ancients called the gods "bonds" or "fetters" (ON *bönd*)—because humans were bound by their power. The most graphic representation of this is the *valknútr*:

This is a magical knot used by Óðinn to bind and liberate. The constellations referred to as the Big and Little Dippers, or the Greater and Lesser Bears, are referred to as wagons or wains in Germanic lore. These northern constellations—which surround the polestar itself—never go below the horizon and are steadily visible and reliably used by navigators over land and sea.

It is well established that Teiwaz was the ancient Germanic god of law, order, and justice. But ancients thought of all conflicts as being resolved by this principle as well, so that war was often called *vapnadómr*, "weapon-judgment." Right was demonstrated though conflict. This remains the guiding principle behind the Anglo-American legal systems where two opposing sides fight out legal cases in a war of words and symbols in the belief that justice will be served in the end.

The names of the days of the week are, as most readers already know, based on the names of our ancestral gods and goddesses—Tuesday is the day of Tīw—the god of justice and law. It is therefore no accident that the American Founding Fathers mandated that elections should be held on his day. Interestingly, the Modern High German word for this day is *Dienstag*, which comes from an older *Dings-tag*—Day of the Thing (i.e., of the Legal Assembly) over which the god of justice would preside.

An important myth about the nature of Teiwaz lies hidden behind the veil of one of his alternate names: Mithotyn. We come across this name in the first book of the *Gesta Danorum* by the Danish mythographer and chronicler Saxo Grammaticus. He recounts that Othin left the land for various reasons, leaving it to Mithotyn—who established new religious cults for the gods wherein each one would be worshipped separately and not as a group. When Othin returned, he deposed Mithotyn and reestablished the common worship of the gods as a collective body. Here we clearly see that Othin (ᚠ) stands for synthesis of various elements, whereas Mithotyn (↑) represents analysis of elements into a rational set of component parts. The Old English name Metod (god) is the same name and etymologically means "the one who metes (i.e., shares or measures) out."

The cosmological role of *teiwaz* seems lost in time. However, this god's transcendent nature does not lend itself to an overabundance of mythic tales. It may have been that he first made the *space* in which creation could take place. The image of his rune is an icon of the process by which a great *pole* is inserted between heaven and earth and as it is raised—as a tent pole separating the material of the tent from the ground below—space is thus created between sky and earth ↑. His abode remains at the top of the pole.

Psychophysiologically, the power of *teiwaz* lies in the continual exercise of *right-doing*, always doing the just thing, always telling the truth, etc. In so acting, an energy is built up in the individual. This energy endows the individual with certain powers the ancients called "luck"—e.g., Old Norse *gæfa*, *hamingja*.

All evidence points in the direction of *teiwaz* being an expression of the transcendental analytical order—the very abstract character of which leads to the god Teiwaz being relegated to relative inactivity in the mythology.

Operatively, *teiwaz* is of great importance in runology. This is the principle which provides order and position to all the elements of the fuþark. This right-order is an essential part of being able to compose and read communications of all sorts, and hence, the meta-communication exercised with runes hinges on this principle.

More overtly in the records of runic inscriptions and literature about runes, we find intriguing clues—all of which indicate the rule of Týr/Tīw as a god of war and victory in war—the Romans interpreted him as Mars. In the Sigrdrífumál (6), we read:

> *Sigrúnar þú skalt kunna,   ef þú vilt sigr hafa,*
> *ok rísta á hjalti hjors,*
> *sumar á véttrimum,   sumar á valböstum,*
> *oc nefna tysvar Tý.*

Victory-runes you shall know,

> if you want to have victory,
> and carve them on the hilt of the sword,

some on the sword-rung,   some on the pommel-plate,

> and name Týr twice.

The ýý-rune was carved on the sword, and the god was invoked twice. In the archeological record, we find an Old English spear where the sign and the symbol of Teiwaz is several times seen as a multiple form, e.g., ↑ or ⇑.

[b]

PGmc. *berkanā* "birch-goddess";
OE *beorc:* "birch";
ON *bjarkan:* "birch" (special rune-name).

The name of this rune is without doubt connected to the word for "birch." However, it is not the ordinary word for this tree, *berkō*. The *-an-ō* suffix indicates a feminine ruler over something, analogous to the masculine suffix *-anaz* in, for example, the name Wōðanaz, literally "inspiration-master." The ordinary Old Norse word for the birch is *björk* < **berkō*. So the Old Norse rune-name *bjarkan* is derived from a form with this special suffix. The OE *beorc* means "birch," but the poetic stanza seems to describe a tree botanically unlike the birch. It says that *beorc* shoots out roots and bears no seed. This has made some identify the OE *beorc* with the poplar tree.[109]

The central principle of *berkanō* is that of the immanent divine—divinity radiating and spreading out within the realm of nature. This is the life force made manifest in the world.

All of the rune-poems emphasize the same idea: the birch is verdant, youthful, vigorous, and beautiful. The teaching of the runic dyads pairs *berkanō* with *teiwaz*—and the final half line invokes the sky: *lyfte ġetenge*: "reaching up to touch the sky." The *málrúnakenningar* reflect these same characteristics emphasizing the idea of the tree radiating or branching out from itself. Many of these references invoke the idea that ᛒ as a symbol of the principle of nature is self-regenerating and that its life force is continuous, that each living thing is contiguous with the next living thing in a genetic paradigm.

One of the disadvantages of recovering the ancient lore surrounding this rune is that it is attached to the feminine divine principle, which at first was especially distasteful to the early Catholic Church. Therefore, much of what we can glean about *berkanō* comes from folklore and popular practices.

The birch is renowned for its early spring foliage, which shimmers with an almost supernatural iridescence. The white bark suggests the bright white skin of the incarnate goddess.

Birch is the renewer of life—it cleanses and invigorates. In some Icelandic cemeteries one can see birch trees placed directly on top of graves.

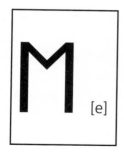

PGmc. *ehwaz*: "horse" (cognate to Lat. equus);
OE *eh*: "war-horse."

The **e**-rune was not used in the Younger Fuþąrk, but the cognate word survives in ON poetry as jór: "stallion."

The main principle of **M** is physical, concrete *power*. This is patently physical in the usual sense, but more importantly, to the ancients it is the secret of a vital force which functions in a way parallel to the physical and one which is also transpersonal as well as personal. The power of *ehwaz* extends the power of man and welds men together into a greater collective force.

Only the OE poem and also lore surrounding the horse in general, and the war-horse of the chieftains in particular, give us direct insight into the inner meaning of *ehwaz*. The OE stanza reads:

(eh) byþ for eorlum   æþelinga wyn,
hors hōfum wlanc,   ðær him hæleþas ymb,
welige on wicgum,   wrixlaþ spræce;
and biþ unstyllum   æfre frōfur.

Horse is the delight of noble-men among the warriors,
a horse high-spirited on its hooves,
where the warriors, who are wealthy in horses, exchange
talk about it, and it is always a benefit to restless men.

Here it is clear that the horse in question is a very valuable one, and one that is respected and treasured by noblemen (*æþelingas*). Why is this so? Two reasons: a horse is a great aid in martial endeavors—the chief occupation of contemporary

Anglo-Saxon noblemen; the horse is also considered a bridge to the other world of the gods. The god Óðinn traveled between the worlds on a horse (Sleipnir—"the Slipper"). Tacitus also reports (*Germania,* chapter 10) that priests practiced a form of divination—learning the will and rede of the gods—from the movements and whinnying of horses.

The *málrúnakenningar* do not help us with regard to lore about the older e-rune, as all references to the /e/ relate to the "pointed" form of the younger i-rune (íss).

Culturally, the importance of the horse cannot be overestimated. The Indo-European-speaking peoples were the first to domesticate the horse, and that development is probably responsible for the fact that Indo-European languages are spoken over four-fifths of the world's landmass. The horse made people mobile over land and reinforced Indo-European ideological principles, which highly valued the ability to move freely, swiftly, and powerfully across broad open spaces. This physical freedom mirrored their ideal of spiritual freedom. When the steppe-dwelling Indo-Europeans met with the ocean, they were motivated by their ideas to create boats and ships which could do for them on water what horses and wagons had done on the land. Again, it is no accident that it was Indo-European speakers who discovered new continents—and even were the first to leave this planet.

Also something of key importance is the level of intimacy developed between horse and rider. They come to act and move as a *unit.* This experience is responsible for the metaphorical extension of the idea of the horse as part of the human psychosomatic complex.

Germanic myth is rich in equine imagery. The two most important examples come from both the heroic and divine mythologies. The greatest of all heroes was Sigurd, who had the most excellent horse of terrestrial existence. His name was Grani ("bearded"). Like Sigurd's sword, Grani was tested against extremes: the horse feared neither water nor fire. Grani's lack of fear of fire allowed Sigurd to penetrate the ring of fire surrounding his *valkyrja*, Sigrdrífa. This access to the summit of Hindarfjell ("Hind-Mountain") gave Sigurd a connection to his higher self—his *fylgja*—and this resulted in his initiation into rune-wisdom. (See Sigrdrífumál in the *Poetic Edda*.) Similarly, Óðinn's mythic steed, Sleipnir, provides access to other dimensions. Sleipnir was born of Loki, who took on female form for this purpose, and the horse is famous for having eight legs—and he is so depicted in Gotlandic art of the ninth century:

This eight-leggedness conceals many meanings: the eight legs of the four pallbearers who carry a corpse to be cremated or buried, or the eight outer-worlds in the cosmic tree structure called Yggdrasill. The name of this tree itself demonstrates its equine association. Yggr is an ancient name of Óðinn meaning "The Terrible," but *drasill* is an old poetic word for "horse." So literally the cosmic tree, the structure for the rational universe, is called the "horse (or mount) of the embodiment of inspiration."

The psychological significance of the horse is further seen in the famous formula: *marr er manns fylgja*, "a horse is a man's soul." Here it is understood that the experience the individual has when riding a horse is analogous to that of the body, or mundane awareness, when it is linked in a harmonious way with the vital powers of the soul.

Ehwaz is a powerful entity that works together with the intellect to make things happen in the world in accord with the plans and dreams of the intellect. This power would be misunderstood if it were relegated to mere "horsepower" alone—rather it is a quasi-spiritual power and repository of such forces which can be inherited from one generation to another.

The horse is an expression of power and also a symbol of the passage between this world and other worlds—often the realm of the dead. Equine symbolism is the most common in pictographic representations found juxtaposed to early runic inscriptions. Runic bracteates often show a man mounted on a horse. This is one of the most common icons in all of early Germanic art. This is usually interpreted as Wōðanaz on his horse. One older inscription, the stone of Eggja (ca. 700), has an abstract horse's head between rows of runic writing, while another, the stone of Roes (ca. 750), has a depiction of a stallion and this image may be referred to in the enigmatic and mysterious text, as interpreted by Magnus Olsen:

ᛁᚾᛞᛁᛏ:ᛉᚱᛉᚤ:

i u þ i n : u d R r A k
jū þin   UddR rak

"horse this UddR drove," i.e., UddR drove this horse

UddR is a proper man's name. The idea of "driving" a horse is an assertion that some magical act (probably a curse) has been committed and is thus *sealed* by the runestone—a sort of certification of the objective reality of the act. This stone was found under the roots of a hazel bush. Most readers probably do not have to be reminded that Egill placed a horse's head on a *níð*-pole made of hazel wood which he erected to drive Erik Bloodaxe out of Norway (*Egil's Saga*, chapter 57).

PGmc. *mannaz:* "human being";
OE *mann:* "human being";
ON *maðr:* "human being (man)."

All sources are unanimous on the name of this rune. It only remains important to focus on the idea that *mannaz* refers to humans of both genders. The English etymology of "woman" shows just how true this was. The word is derived from the compound *wīf-mann*: "woman-person."

The central principle of *mannaz* is the complete nature of man: mortality, consciousness, culture. That is, man is a conscious being (as a result of the divine gifts),[110] who must profitably interact with others of his kind to thrive and enjoy life, and in the end he is mortal. Man is the ordinary presence of the divine in Midgard.

The rune-poems are all remarkably similar in the message they convey. Man is called the "joy of man"—*maðr er manns gaman* in the Old Icelandic Rune-Poem, and a similar sentiment comes through in the first part of the stanza of the Old English Rune-Poem for *mann*. But all also insist on man's mortality, calling man the "increase or augmentation of the soil" (*moldar auki*)—i.e., when the body is buried after death.

The *málrúnakenningar* generally support all of this lore, and add some things of a profoundly philosophical nature about humanity—calling the /m/ both "book-learning's blender" and *raunabot*, "the true or real bettering," i.e., "improvement." This all points to the most powerful and important aspect of humanity—its indwelling divine *potential*.

It is most likely that *mannaz* is etymologically related to the word for "thinking," i.e., that man is the thinking being. Tacitus (*Germania*, chapter 2) says that the Germans have a god named Mannus, which is likely the same word as *mannaz*. In other words, the ancient Germanic peoples recognized the inherent divine qualities in man.

This idea of divinity in man is well-supported in the mythology otherwise as well. The essential mystery of ᛗ is the mystery of mankind—how it came to be and what its true character is. These questions are answered in the tradition of the *Edda* in the Völuspá (stanzas 17–18), where we read:

> Uns þrír kómu   úr því liði,
> öflgir ok ástgir,   æsir, at húsi:
> fundu á landi,   litt megandi,
> Ask ok Emblu,   ørlöglausa.
>
> Önd þau ne áttu,   óð þau ne höfðu,
> lá né læti   né litu góða:
> önd gaf Óðinn,   óð gaf Hœnir,
> lá gaf Lóðurr   ok litu góða.

Then there came to the coast three from the host, mighty and powerful Æsir, they found Ask and Embla (= Ash and Elm) on the land, with little power and lacking fates.

They did not have spirit, they did not have inspiration, neither did they have vital warmth nor voice, nor good coloring: Óðinn gave spirit, Hœnir gave inspiration, Lóðurr gave vital warmth and good coloring.

These stanzas establish three great traditional truths: 1) proto-humanity was a preexisting organic being evolved in nature; 2) true humanity is created by the endowment of the preexisting organic matrix with spiritual or formal gifts from a triad of gods; and 3) humanity is a complex entity resulting from the intersection of the earthly and divine. In no other ancient mythology of mankind is this pattern made more pointedly explicit. Postmodern "space-brother mythology" is merely an atavism for this deep ancestral pattern of thought. The idea that man was created by the interbreeding of humanoid earth-apes and extra-terrestrial beings is merely the latest version of the myth.

When it comes to understanding the cultural implications of *mannaz*, we are confronted with a paradox. *Mannaz* is not a cultural object in essence,[111] but rather the very subject of culture, i.e., *mannaz* is the creator and definer of culture.

This is no mere philosophical speculation. The etymological use of the root *mann-* in Old Norse and Old English demonstrates clearly that the ancients understood the role of *mannaz* as the cultural creator. In Old Norse we find the verb *menna*, "to make a man," in reflexive use "to become a man" and the participle of this verb, *menntr*: "bred; accomplished as a man." We also see *mennta*: "to civilize." But most importantly, there is the word *menning*, which first basically means "breeding," i.e., not merely the biological process, but also the process of education and training we call culture. In Modern Icelandic the word *menning* means "culture." Old English has the word *mann-þeaw*: "a manner, custom, practice." This is a compound of *mann* and *þeaw*: "usage, practice, mode of conduct." So that *mann-þeaw* is what we really understand as culture, as such. It is clearly through *mannaz* that culture is handed down, and it is upon *mannaz* which the cultivation of culture is dependent.

Cosmologically, the importance of ᛘ is that the gods have made themselves manifest and incarnate in the material universe—within matter the gods (*reginn*) can both experience reality and in*form* it with consciousness. This is the cosmic purpose of man: to give the gods experience and to implement the pattern of consciousness in the material universe (Midgard).

From the foregoing it should be obvious that *mannaz* is the psychophysiological mystery par excellence. It describes the process by which man was endowed with divine qualities and the general structure of those qualities. Óðinn (Wōðanaz) gives önd (spirit), by which divine consciousness enters the proto-human. Hœnir (Wīli) provides óðr (the principle and form of divine inspiration, or mind derived from the next higher level, Óðinn). Similarly, Lóðurr (Wīhaz) gives *lá* and *litr* (aesthetic—divine—shape and form) based on the influx from the next highest form, Hœnir. In reality these are three aspects of the same god who has never been known by merely one name alone. (See the Grímnismál in the *Poetic Edda*.)

Viewed from the testimony of traditional sources, it is clear that the principle underlying *mannaz* is that of potential godlike consciousness made manifest in the world. Without this rune, the runes themselves could never be known in Midgard.

Operatively, the **m**-rune signifies in a symbolic way the operator, the subject or performer, of every act of so-called magic. When a god such as Óðinn appears in the mythology to perform an act of magic, in fact it is a direct action imposed by the subjective universe of Óðinn upon whatever object is delineated. In myth this appears as an act of magic because mythic language is one of image and action, not so much philosophical discourse, When a ᛬ᛘ᛬ successfully operates magically, he or she is 1) fulfilling at least for that moment a divine state of being, and 2) is acting in a way analogous to Óðinn or other gods who act upon the universe. This analogous action by :ᛗ: is only *possible* because of the structural and qualitative similarities between the gods and :ᛗ:. These similarities are a result of the divine gifts imparted by the triadic god, Óðinn.

[l]

PGmc. *laguz:* "liquid";
OE *lagu:* "sea, water";
ON *lögr:* "sea; liquid."

All sources appear to be in agreement as to the word which provides this rune-name. Wolfgang Krause speculated that the original name of the rune was actually *laukaz*, not *laguz*, due to the frequent use of the former in older runic inscriptions. This opened the door to more comprehensive meditations on the possibility that each rune, each *mystery*, had at least three different names. This line of thought led to the development of a listing of possible alternate rune-names printed as appendix B in the book. Despite the unanimity on the rune-name, *laguz* does not provide the usual term for water or "sea" in any of the Germanic dialects—it appears to have acquired these precise meanings later, over time. Its original precise meaning is not easy to determine at first.

Despite these apparent challenges, we will see that *laguz* refers to the original liquid state of one pole of the manifesting universe. The other pole is, of course, characterized by *fire*.

Laguz is the archetype of liquid, and so lends its name to both water and sea. Water is the vivifying essence and vital matrix of life in all its infinite possibilities.

All of the rune-poems refer to water in one form or another with several aspects of it emphasized. The Old English Rune-Poem indicates the vastness and volatility of the great ocean water as men try to guide ships across it, while the Old Icelandic Rune-Poem points to water boiling, and belonging to a wide kettle. The Old Norse Rune-Rhyme shows water being again very dynamic as it falls from a mountain in the form of a waterfall. In his *Altnordisches etymologisches Wörterbuch*, Jan de Vries indicates that the word probably originally indicated specifically "warm water"—used in brewing, etc.[112] This fits with the underlying consistent reference in the poems to the dynamism of the water in question, "tossing sea," "swirling stream," (water) falling from a mountain. This water is anything but tranquil or still.

The *málrúnakenningar* provide a storehouse of interesting and nuanced lore about ᛁᛚᛁ. Reflective of the most ancient Germanic cosmological lore, it calls the magical letter /l/ both *Ymis blóð* ("Ymir's blood") and *landabelti* ("the belt of lands"). The former refers to the idea that water on earth was first created from the blood of Ymir when Óðinn sacrificed him; the latter speaks to the concept that the entirety of Midgard is surrounded by a belt of water, or ocean, which encircles all lands. The /l/ is also called the "fetter (or restricter) of liars." This is a direct reference to the ancient Germanic legal usage of the ordeal by water[113] to discover those who bear false witness in legal proceedings. It is also called the *humra-kvöld* ("twilight evening"), which references the old concept of the west as a direction of infinite sea and *þröngvasti kostur* ("most difficult choice"), which in a related way points to the vast ocean of the west as the greatest test of man's courage and resolve.

This exposes an important cultural aspect connected to water and the sea. It is often missed that the sea is more of a highway than a barrier. The Germanic peoples had their particular ethnogenesis in the present-day Danish archipelago and the coastal regions of southern Sweden and northern Germany—in other words, areas all very close to the sea. We can observe that they were to a great extent the developmental inheritors of the Indo-European Bronze Age culture in this region. The rock art of these people betrays a ship- and boat-based culture.

The sea becomes an ever more efficient surface over which to travel, culminating in the Viking Age (800–1100) with its seafaring to North America in the west and along rivers to the Caspian Sea and Persia in the east. But the waterways and navigation upon them were always a challenge and a danger to men.

Mythically, important aquatic figures in the northern cycles are the "giant" Ægir and the sea goddess Rán. Rán is sometimes called Ægir's daughter and sometimes his wife. Ægir plays a great role as the host at divine banquets—the settings of the Lokasenna and Grímnismál poems. He possesses great brewing kettles beloved by the gods.[114] His very name means simply "water (man)"—cognate to the Latin Aquarius. His daughters are said to be nine in number, and embody the waves of the sea. Rán, whose name means "robber," presumably because the sea robs so many families of their young men, is said to have a net with which she catches those who die by drowning and who then go to her realm below the sea rather than to Hel or Valhöll.[115]

In the realm of cosmology, the watery world is often missed when the original cosmic dichotomy of fire and water (Gylfaginning sect. 4) is ignored in favor of a subsequent contrast between fire (or sparks from fire) and ice (= frozen water). But the proto-cosmic contrast was actually between fire and water in liquid form, and it is noticed that water is the only substance which expands as it is frozen—showing its unique properties. In the re-created cosmos, water is said to have come from the blood of the giant Ymir. This water now circulates throughout the whole cosmic order as a life-giving liquid.

Both the cosmological and mythic references to water and the sea show how bound up this substance of liquidity is with questions of life, death, and immortality. The liquids within the human body and their contained, yet warm and pulsating, circulation—along with inflows and expulsions of liquid substances of various kinds—all define and describe life in the body. Liquids of various name flow through the body as water flows in rivers—especially subterranean courses tapped into by wells and springs.

Laguz is not merely "water," but liquid substances of all kinds. It is the very principle of liquidity which acts as the *matrix* (Latin for "womb") for the development and manifestation of life.

The most conspicuous use of the l-rune in actual runic inscriptions centers on the terms *laukaz* (leek) and *līn* (flax or linseed). The word *laukaz* is frequently used as a magical word-formula and is found on bracteates. Both *laukaz* and *līn* refer to magically important plants, and they both seem to indicate a sexual component—*laukaz*, a masculine principle, and *līn* (flax), a feminine one. The leek grows up in a phallic manner from the ground. It is white and pure in the midst of the dark earth, thrusts upward in the spring with a verdant vertical stalk, and blooms out into an array of many small white flowers. The flax plant is sacred to Freyja; its seeds provide health benefits; and from the fibers of its stalks linen cloth is produced.

One mysterious inscription, the bone tanning knife of Gjervik (Norway, ca. 450 CE), bears a series of ten l-runes in a row. These may stand for *laukaz* × 10, or more likely, it refers to the fertility-giving formula *līn – laukaz* × 5.

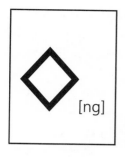

[ng]

PGmc. *ingwaz:* "earth-god";

OE *Ing:* "earth-god," or a culture hero named Ing.

This rune is not found in the Younger Fuþąrk, but the name survives in Old Norse onomastics (study of names). There are many personal names constructed with this element, e.g., Inga, Ingiborg, Ingimarr, as well as the divine formula Ingvi-Freyr. The Swedes are said to be descended from this god/hero, as can be seen the *Ynglingasaga* (i.e., saga of the descendants of Ing).

Although this rune-name is clearly a direct reference to an extremely ancient name of a god, the Old English word *ing* meaning "a meadow" must have been evocative of the idea that Ing was a god of fertility. The word is so ancient that a convincing etymology has eluded scholars. Ing was already known by this name in the first century, as reflected by Tacitus's report about the *Ing-vaeones*—one of the three divisions of the ancient Germanic tribes and the one found next to the sea. (And in the rune-row we also find Ing next to, and paired with, the sea :l:!

Fundamentally, *ingwaz* is the embodied seed principle of organic growth, fertility, and well-being. From it grows the possibilities of eternal renewal among the gods and among men.

The Old English Rune-Poem is our only direct literary piece of evidence about the lore surrounding this rune. Other clues are contained in the study of names, linguistics, and contemplation of the unique significance of this rune's shape. The older *ingwaz* appears in many variations, e.g., ◇○□. It is usually executed in a manner indicative of an intention to make the stave smaller than others and higher off of any implied lower edge of a line along which the runestaves are being inscribed. Its original shape was probably a small circle. This has led us to speculate that it is emblematic of a "heavenly seed" of the principle of a cyclical process itself.

In the OERP, Ing is said to originate among the "East-Danes," by which the Swedes might be indicated—i.e., those descendants of Yngvi-Freyr. Ing is also called a *hæle(þ)*: "warrior," not a god per se, although Ing is certainly originally a god-form. (In the Middle Ages it was common to "demote" pagan gods to the level of mere mortals.) The wagon (*wēn*, more usual form *wæġn*) is most probably a reference to the constellation we know as the Big Dipper, called a "wagon" by the Germanic peoples.

The *málrúnakenningar* are of no help here, since the use of a separate letter for the sound [ng] essentially disappeared with the demise of the Older Fuþark and the Old English Fuþorc.

Ingwaz is an archaic mythological name for the god of the earth. This is not to say that he is the embodiment of the Earth herself—that distinction belongs to Jörð (Earth)—called both an Áss and a giantess in the old texts. Rather Ing is a god of the land—soil—in juxtaposition to the water. (Hence perhaps the pairing of ᛚ ᛬ ◇.) Culturally this makes Ing the god of farming and fertility of fields and crops. It seems that Ing is a god who dies and is resurrected, just as in the world of vegetative life there is a cycle of life, apparent death, and renewal. The wagon referred to in the OERP likely signifies a wagon used to transport the souls of the dead to another world, whence they are to be reborn. This wagon is reflected in the stars. De Vries points to the many graves from archaic times which contain a wagon or chariot.[116]

Mythically, it must be said that Ingwaz seems to have fallen together with the god known in the North as "the Lord," i.e., Freyr. It appears most likely that Ingwaz was the archaic name of the god of the bounties of the earth, and Freyr was one of his later titles in Scandinavia. In the *Ynglingasaga* (See *Heimskringla* I.23), a definite link is made between Yngvi, Freyr, and the legendary king Fróði, who ruled in Denmark at the time of great peace and prosperity. In the Old Norse Rune-Rhyme, this is remembered with the verse: *Ár er gumna góði, get ek at örr var Fróði*, "Harvest is the profit of men, I understand that Fróði was generous."

Cosmologically, the principle of *ingwaz* is that of the seed or kernel. It is the small container of compact information which, under the right conditions and in the right environment, will replicate itself as a greater transformed object, which in turn replicates itself cyclically. The icon of the rune :◇: is the seed, which is broken open to grow its fruit in :◇:. This seed principle is that by which living things gain transformational immortality.

In the esoteric physiology of :ᛜ:, it is the secret of semen— how the father plants his seed forth to carry on his name, or how it can be retained for his own heroic immortality. We know that the Indo-European peoples knew the role of the father in the process of reproduction, because they used a patrilineal form of descent and inheritance. (Any reasonably careful observation of the reproductive process, even among their dogs and horses, would have quickly informed them of this reality.)

:◇: is the seed principle at work in the world and in all realms of being. The principle is seen in nature but reflected in the symbolic and spiritual realms as well as an essence hidden away, where it might gestate and bring forth fruit in forms such as events and manifestations.

In the operative model of rune-magic, the principle behind :◇: is essential. Runes are concealed, buried, hidden, just as seeds are planted that they may fulfill their secret purposes and spring forth transformed into useful products in the "future."

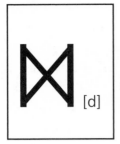

PGmc. *dagaz:* "day";
OE *dæġ:* "day."
The **d**-rune is not found in the Younger Fuþạrk, but the word dagr: "day" is the common ON term for "day"—the whole period of time from one sunset to the next.

There is universal consensus that *dagaz* was the original name of the **d**-rune. Words derived from the Proto-Germanic root *dag-* provide additional insight into the nuances of the name. There is a verb *daga*: "to dawn," from which the noun *dagan*: "dawn" is derived. The compound *dagsmörk*: "day-marks" indicates the traditional division of the day into eight parts. Another word derived from the same root (by the phenomenon of *ablaut*) is *dægn* or *dægr*, which indicates one half of a day— one being light, the other dark. The term *dægra-skipti* denotes the twilight or both morning and evening.[117]

The principle of *dagaz* is the polarity of light and darkness and the synthesis of them that comes at twilight. This principle is applied to all things and creates the first model or paradigm of paradox.

Our only poetic description of the **d**-rune occurs in the Old English Rune-Poem. There its divine heritage is referenced as it is called a "sending" (OE *sand* or *sond*) of the "lord" (OE *drihten*) and *Metodes leoht* ("creator's light"). The word *sand* can also mean a "message" or even "messenger." Its connection with light is affirmed and its universally beneficial effects are emphasized. It is good for all, rich and poor alike.

The *málrúnakenningar* do not help us unravel anything more about the old **d**-rune as almost all of them clearly refer to the icon of the pointed **t**-rune of the medieval period. These allude to the god Týr—especially to his encounter with Fenrir, the loss of his hand, and so on.

Cultural features connected with the word *dagaz/dagr/dæg* are numerous. The key cultural tradition which allows for insight into the inner analysis of *dagaz* is the way in which the day was divided up in the ancient North—into eight divisions called *mál*: "times" or *mörk*: "marks."

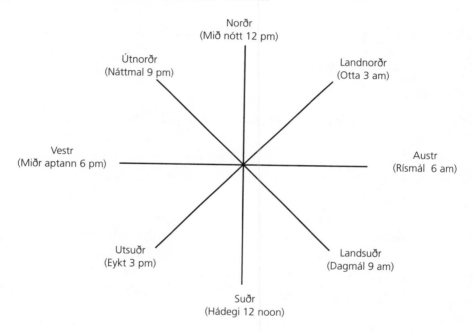

The day was divided into eight parts, as were the directions in the sky, which were called ættir—as were, of course, the runes.

The iconic appearance of the ᛬ᛞ᛬ rune is suggestive of *doubling*, corroborated by the double meaning of *dagaz*, being both light and dark. If the double structure ▷ ◁ is only code for a deeper reduplication, the rune may have been a representation of the division of the day:

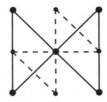

Often ignored in discussions of the **d**-rune is the fact that Dagr is a figure in Norse myth. The familiar invocation of Sigrdrí-fumál 3: *Heill Dagr, heilir Dags synir. . .*: "Hail Day, hail the sons of Day . . ." is easily interpreted as meaning that Dagr is a god or demigod. Simek gives Dagr an entry in his *Dictionary* which reads in part:

> The personified day. Snorri understands Dagr to be this when he calls him the son of Nótt "night" and of Del-lingr. . . . Snorri also mentions that Dagr is the ancestor of the line of the Döglingar, to which the hero Helgi Hundingsbani, who is in turn killed by a certain Dagr in a possibly cultic context, also belongs. [Otto] Höfler deduced from the existence of Dagr and the Döglingar a mythological figure *Daguz, whom he considered to have been a personification of day and of light and was venerated by the Suebi.[118]

Obviously, the ᛞ has cosmological import. It describes the hidden patterns behind cyclical processes. The day is bounded by dawn and dusk, the day is divided into light and dark. The components if this cycle play out for all to see. They play out over ages, hidden from the sight of all but the wise by their enormity.

Anything which is born, has life, only to pass away to a new beginning is governed by the process described by ᛞ. This includes the human organism and its constituent parts. At differ-ent stages of development the organism is provided with different essences, which result from the cyclical process working on basic innate components. The two challenges in this is to be able to vitalize the night-side with light (essence from the light-side), while at the same time accepting and absorbing the essence produced in the night-side itself.

Underlying the **d**-rune is the general principle of the delimited confines of a cyclical process. The day bordered by the horizontal polarity of dawn (OE *dægung*) and dusk (OE *dux*).[119] Day is a delimiting of time (motion) within a polarized model.

Among the rune-shapes of the Older Fuþark, the ᛟ is at once the most complex and ideographically loaded of all. It is a peculiar configuration. Definite and recognizable, it is at the same time enigmatic, and dare we say *paradoxical*. Although it could be said that the ᛟ is a reduplicated epigraphical Roman D = ▷ → ▷ + ◁ = ᛟ, it is more likely that it is an inherited ideogram reaching back at least into the Bronze Age. Its image describes the nuances and paradoxes of its name. From an operative perspective, it provides a key to the paradoxical state of consciousness necessary for both reading (understanding) and writing (operating) runes.

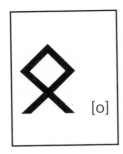

PGmc. *ōþala:* "inherited property";
OE *éþel:* "one's own property, inheritance, country, home; native country."
This rune is lacking in the Younger Fuþark, however the word is found as ON *óðal:* "nature, quality, property; property held in allodial tenure; one's native land, homeland, inheritance."

[o]

There are few controversies surrounding this rune-name and its basic meaning. The rune was frequently used in Anglo-Saxon manuscripts to stand for the Old English word *éþel* or *œþel*, meaning "homeland, country," etc. Besides *óðal*, another Old Norse word derived from PGmc. *ōþala* is *æði ~ œði:* "nature, disposition; mind; manners." This is a neuter noun. Its masculine form fell together with ON *óðr:* "inspiration; rage." These derived forms, as well as others having to do with descriptions of genetic kinfolk, e.g., Old Frisian *ēdila*, "great grandfather," show that the concept underlying this word is related to genetic descent and natural connections between people. This is why and how it came to mean nature itself (Ice. *eðli*). *Ōþala* is the tribal concept, and secondarily, it is applied to the land or space occupied by the tribe, or "homeland."

The principle of *ōþala* is that of containment within borders or limits—the existence of lines of demarcation. The tribe has its definition—you are in it or outside of it. These limitations are necessary for all growth and development. All models belonging to the paradigm [inner : outer] belong to *ōþala*.

Because the ᛟ rune was omitted from the Younger Fuþark, the Norse poems do not refer to it. The *málrúnakenningar* are likewise silent, as the /o/ letters all refer to a derivative of the old a-rune, which became medieval /o/, *ōs*, usually meaning "waterway, river mouth." The OERP tells us what we need to know:

(éþel) byþ oferléof　　　　*ǣghwylcum men,*
gif hē mōt ðǣr rihtes　　　*and gerysena on*
brūcan on bolde　　　　　　*blēadum oftast.*

Homeland is much praised　　by every man,
if there he may enjoy　　　　what is right and fitting
in his own home　　　　　　most often in prosperity.

Here we see that *ēþel* is good for every man (rich or poor) and that people are aware of its goodness; hence, it is praised. Three qualities require attention and will provide benefit within the homeland *if* people attend to them: *riht* (right, justice), *ġerysene* (propriety, higher culture), and *blǣd* (prosperity). A happy life is ensured for everyone by these principles being cultivated and balanced. Justice is an ancient concept and one much developed by the Germanic peoples—the English Common Law system is derived from it. Within the homeland, right is practiced—without it there are no guarantees. *Ġerysene* is an interesting word and concept. It is derived from the verb *risan*: "to rise." That which is *risen up*, made lofty, elevated in quality. This denotes the higher ethics and practices of tribal members which describe an inner state of principled existence and an outer practice of disciplined behavior. Prosperity, and the happiness which comes with it, will follow.

Culturally, no rune can be more loaded with meaning than *ōþala*. The meaning of *ōþala* as a defining mechanism provides for tribal (or group) *identity*. There are insiders and outsiders. These definitions may be biological (family descent), linguistic (common language), ideological (ritual connections by marriage vows or oaths sworn), or a host of other things. But group identity is essential for human happiness and well-being.

Within the confines of the ring described by ᛟ, there exists a sovereign power. This power allows for operation within the ring as well as protection of the ring and its contents from outside invaders—physical or moral. Sovereignty involves ownership of land, institutions, and so on. The Germanic king owned his land as an individual man. Other Indo-European peoples, such as the Celts, owned land collectively. The tribe owned it, not the king. But the Germanic ideology of individual ownership of things is the best system for preserving tribal *freedom* because it places full responsibility on one individual.

These concepts hinge on, and in turn reinforce, the basic idea of ᛉ defining limits or borders within which certain values and practices are cultivated and shielded.

The greater border, or "property line," is found at the edges of tribal or group allegiance. (This later gave rise to the idea of "national borders.") This is where one set of laws began and another ended. Hence, to be cast out of a group space was to be an out-law—outside the value system of one's own group.

The innermost such borders are found within the confines of the whole, and they define sacred spaces. Sacred space is separated from profane space by a line of demarcation created by a symbolic physical barrier—a ring of stones, wooden poles, etc. Often a rope was strung between wooden stakes to mark off such sacred enclosures for juridical parliaments or religious functions. The rope was called the *vébönd*.[120] Obviously, the use of rope and stakes allowed the space to be moved from place to place. The important thing was that the concept inner : outer, sacred : profane existed and was *used* in an effort to build and perpetuate a strong culture.

In the mythology of the North, there are examples of cosmic spaces with strong barriers demarcating an inner : outer model. Most conspicuous are Ásgarðr and Miðgarðr. The element *garðr* in their names indicates that they are seen as *enclosures*. Old farmsteads typically were fenced in with wicker barriers. Ásgarðr is envisioned as a fortress with impenetrable walls. It is related in the myth of the Master-Builder, who fashioned the stone stronghold of Ásgarðr, that its wall would be "so excellent that it would be safe and secure against cliff-giants and frost ogres" (*Edda*, chapter 41).

The references in mythology to enclosed spaces as safe havens for the sentient beings of the cosmos—gods and men—point to the cosmological and psychophysical realities of ᛜ. In the cosmic and social order, the concept of space set apart and protected from outside interference is essential to order and prosperity. The separate space is, in our most ancient terminology, *wīh-hailag*—sacrosanct. The act of separating one kind of space from another is to make it *wīh*: "holy or sacred." The space then is filled with sanctified power and becomes *hailag*: "holy, sanctified."[121]

In the psychophysiology of man, ᛜ defines not only the borders or boundaries between the individual and his natural and social context, but also the lines between various organic groups of people—families, clans, trines, and nations—and their environments. To the ancients, in their wisdom, there were always certain rituals or rites for moving from one "space" or "category" to another. That the space or categories first *exist* and are to be strengthened is supported first, then awareness of the right ways for these holy categories to interact productively is essential.

Among the most ancient runic inscriptions is one that perfectly illustrates the meaning of ᛜ on several levels: the Ring of Piatroassa. I discuss this object at some length in my book *The Mysteries of the Goths*. The inscription reads:

ᚷᚢᛏᚫᚻᛁᛜᚹᛁᚾᚫᛁᛚᚫᚷ

gutaniowihailag

Gutani ᛜ *wih-hailag*

Goths' ᛜ sacrosanct

This neck- or arm-ring functioned as a crown or sign of sovereignty, for a Gothic king or chieftain. The object, a ring, and the rune ᛜ, illustrate the principle inscribed: *wīh-hailag*—to be set apart and filled with power.

With *ōþala* we come to the end of the Older Fuþark system. In what follows we will continue in the same format and discuss the qualities of the nine additional runes used at one time or another by the Anglo-Saxons.

A NOTE ON THE ANGLO-FRISIAN EXTENSION TO THE RUNIC SYSTEM

As previously discussed, the North Sea region saw a systematic extension to the twenty-four rune system. Runes were simply added on to the previous system, with several phonetic changes being made to the values of the initial twenty-four. These changes were determined by sound developments in the languages in which these runes were used, i.e., Anglo-Saxon and Frisian. Most notably the fourth rune goes from [a] to [o], with a modification in the form of the rune from ᚠ to ᚩ. What is clear is that the extension from twenty-four to thirty-three runic characters did not occur all at once. There was an early organic phase and a later antiquarian phase.

The first phase occurred as early as the great Anglo-Saxon migration from northern Germany and southern Jutland to present-day England in the mid-fifth century. Our best piece of evidence for this is the Undley bracteate (ca. 500 CE) which was the distinctive ᚩ-rune. The Thames sax shows the extension most scholars believe was representative of this earlier first phase: ᚪ ᚩ ᚨ ᚣ, a, æ, y, ea.

Somewhat later additional runes, ᛡ [io], ᛢ [q], ᛣ [k], ᛥ [st], and ᛤ [g], were added. These latter runes rarely occur in actual inscriptions. Most seem limited to antiquarian manuscripts. However, the names and ordering of the runes in question indicate that those responsible for shaping the system were aware of the mythic and symbolic importance of the runes, even if they were now being made to serve a more eclectic and multiethnic code.

One peculiarity which should be noted is that the **io**-rune appears to have belonged to this later phase of runic innovation, although a stanza relating to it has been inserted between the **y**- and **ea**-runes in the Old English Rune-Poem. This is suggestive of the possibility that poetic stanzas also existed for the **q**-, **k**-, **st**-, and **g**-runes as well.

These notes, although they were scholarly in tone, are intended to provide background material for operative runologists who choose to write their formulas in English runes—especially using the modern English language.

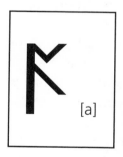

[a]

PGmc. *aik-:* "oak tree";
OE *āc:* "oak tree";
ON *eik:* "oak; tree in general."

The name is only used to designate the OE rune ᚪ. It clearly refers to the oak (*Quercus robur*). A word derived from PGmc. *aik-* is used universally among the Germanic languages for this tree, but it seems to be a term restricted to Germanic dialects. In Iceland oaks were unknown, so the term was applied to trees in general—this is because the oak is considered the tree of all trees.

The oaken principle is well-known: it stands for steadfastness, strength in adversity, and hardiness. It is a natural sign of loyalty and truth.

Two separate aspects of Northern oak lore are alluded to in the OERP. First, it is said that *on land* it is known that its fruit—the acorn—is used as feed for pigs. But *on the water* it is used as the building material for the best ships, and that in stormy seas the "loyalty" (OE *treow*), that is, dependability, of the oaken construction is tested.

The oak is culturally important in the Germanic world, both symbolically and practically. In the practical sense, the oak is the best building material. Oaken beams provided the best superstructures for halls and homes. As the OERP hints at, this wood was also the best for making ships and boats.

The oak was relatively more important to the mythic lives of the South or West Germanic peoples—the Continental Germans—than it was in Scandinavia. The most famous single oak of German antiquity is the *robur jovis* (Oak of Jupiter), which the evangelist Boniface had cut down near Geismar at the beginning of the eighth century.[122] This oak was presumably sacred to Þunor (Thor), as Jupiter was the *interpretatio Romana* of Thor. (The Romans, and subsequently their Christian followers, called the Germanic gods by the names of their own gods according to an ancient and set system, e.g., Mercurius = Odin, Mars = Tyr, Jupiter = Thor). Botanists have discovered that lightning strikes oaks more than any other tree.[123] Holy oaks continued to be venerated in northern Germany even after official Christianization. Near Minden young people of both sexes were said to dance around a holy oak with shouts of joy every Easter. There was a solemn annual procession to a holy oak in the region of Paderborn.[124]

In the psychophysiological realm, the oak is a natural manifestation of the steadfast power of the will and the unrelenting force of courage in the face of adversity.

These general principles are seen in man's environment and are honored and given due worship in the lives of men.

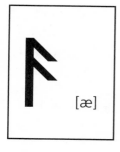

[æ] **PGmc**. *askaz:* "ash tree";
OE *æsc:* "ash tree";
ON *askr:* "ash tree."

As a rune-name this word only appears in the Old English tradition. The PGmc. word *askaz* also results in ON *askr*. The ash (Lat. *fraxinus*) is important culturally and symbolically.

The principle of *askaz* is strength and steadfastness under threat of destruction.

The OERP describes the ash tree in natural and culturally symbolic terms. It is seen as lofty, strong and steadfast, and dear to men. But despite its being so beloved, it is often "attacked." This idea that it is embattled: *him feohtan on firas monige*, "many men fight against it," is most likely a reference to the fact that mostly ash was used to fashion spear shafts. The most typical such spear was a long thrusting lance, not a throwing spear. This weapon was the first to engage the enemy and was used both as a thrusting and slashing weapon.

The ash is described in some ways that are similar to the oak—and the runes are also similar in shape and sound. Ash wood too was used for making ships and boats as well as small bowls for eating and drinking. Old Norse *askr* was a term of liquid measure equaling the contents of four such bowls.[125]

Mythically, there are two overriding corollaries to the ash-rune, i.e., the idea that the World-Tree (Yggdrasill) is called an ash, and that the first human male was named Askr (Ash).

Yggdrasill is repeatedly called an ash, although this cosmic tree may have also been envisioned as a yew—as evidenced by the fact that the great tree at Uppsala was a yew and that Yggdrasill is at one point referred to as a *barr-askr*, "needle-ash"[126] which indicates a coniferous tree. In any event, the word *askr* seems to have been symbolically important as a designation of the cosmic tree. It will be noted that this tree is said to be under constant attack—from worms gnawing at its roots, to harts devouring its leaves.[127] So the statement about the ash being attacked in the OERP may be an oblique reference to the cosmic tree as well.

The first humans were fashioned from pieces of wood (i.e., evolution took place from a vegetative to an animal level of life)—presumably from ash and elm trees, man and woman, respectively. Askr is the name of the first man endowed by the gods with the spiritual and aesthetic gifts which define the human being. The first man was formed from the same material which defines the cosmic order: Askr is a reflection of the World-Ash. By the same token, we can assume that man is under constant attack by forces analogous to those which gnaw at the cosmic tree. The roots of the tree, like the roots of humanity, are nourished by the waters of Urðarbrunnr, by which we mean *the results of virtuous and/or heroic action in the world*.

Although the dyadic systems present in the Older Fuþark cannot be said to have extended in any systematic way to the Anglo-Frisian Fuþorc, ; and a do seem to reflect a dyad with steadfastness being the principle which binds them together.

[ȳ]

PGmc. *eihwaz:* "yew";
OE *ȳr:* "yew bow";
ON *ýr:* "yew bow."

The name of this Old English rune is also reflected in that of the sixteenth rune of the Younger Fuþark and the thirteenth rune of the Older Fuþark. Just as ash might mean a tree or a spear, the shaft of which was so typically made of ash that the name of the wood came to stand for the weapon, in the same way "yew" became synonymous with the bow.

The principles of reliability are emphasized in the first three runes of the Anglo-Frisian extension of the system: ᚪ - ᚫ - ᚣ. The oak and ash demonstrate steadfastness and strength of essence, while the yew bow expresses the reliability of an instrument used to enforce the will over long distances. The bow launches the implied, and here invisible, *arrow*. The principle is reliable instrumentality.

Our sources for lore extend beyond the OERP in this instance because the Old Icelandic Rune-Poem also refers to the meaning of *yew* in terms of a bow. The OERP tells us that ᚣ is a joy (ᚹ) and honor to nobles and warriors, and that it is beautiful on a horse (ᛗ). Why is it a joy? Because it is *fæstlic on færelde,* "reliable on an expedition." Besides defining ýr as a "bent bow," the OIRP also says that it is the *fífu fárbauti,* which literally means something like "the arrow's giant." The word used for "giant" here is *fárbauti,* "harm-striker."[128] The *málrúnakennin-gar* provide evidence that ýr (ý) had become so identified as a bow that it was transferred to another type of wood used to make bows, i.e., the elm. Describing the magical letter /y/, the *málrúnakenningar* use the kennings *uppdreginn álmur*, "pulled-up elm tree"; *bentur bogi*, "bent bow"; and *spentur álmur*, "a drawn elm-bow."

The bow was well-known as a weapon at least as far back as the Bronze Age. Rock carvings in Sweden made in the first millennium BCE show several examples of the bow and arrow, and this weapon continues to be used right up through medieval times.

In the Anglo-Saxon Age, the bow and arrow were mainly used for hunting, although the OERP calls them *fydgeatewa sum*, "a kind of war-gear."

In mythology, the bow and arrow were famously mastered by the god Ullr, who was also known to be an expert skier and skater. This god was especially worshipped in Sweden.

Symbolically, the bow and arrow combination is powerful. It shows that with the right materials, coupled with mindful effort, it is possible to project the will of the individual over long distances and effect the aims of that will.

[ea]

PGmc. *auraz:* "wet clay, mud, wet soil";
OE *ear:* "earth, soil";
ON *aurr:* "mud, wet soil."

This is only known as a runestave in the Old English system, of course. However, the other languages give additional clues as to the importance of ᛇ.

As the note at the beginning of this section indicated, *ear* is the concluding rune of the oldest extension of the Anglo-Frisian Fuþorc. It therefore touches upon the idea of finality. The general principle of ᛇ is that of a return to base form, a return to a chaotic mass out of which new beginnings are possible.

Besides the name and its cognates in other Germanic languages, our only source for lore surrounding *ear* is the stanza of the OERP. It speaks of *ear* as the soil in an inhumation grave—and that such is loathsome (*egle*) to every warrior (*eorl*). It speaks of the process of decay, as the body is consumed by the soil. Here we have an echo of the focus on mortality found in all stanzas relating to the **m**-rune—e.g., *maðr er moldar auki*, "man is the increase of earth" (OIRP). But most importantly, the OERP stanza provides three dimensions of decay:

fruits fall	—	*bleda gedreosaþ*
joys depart	—	*wynna gewitaþ*
pledges fail	—	*wæra geswicaþ*

There is organic, emotional, and moral decay that comes with death.

Burial practices among the Germanic peoples varied over time and place. In the oldest times cremation appears to have been widely practiced—a custom of Indo-European origin. However, inhumation burials were also known. Most early inhumations were rich graves with opulent grave goods—but they lacked weapons. This does not mean they were pacifistic, merely that their particular tribal, clanic, or cultic custom did not include this ritual component. Funerary style in pagan times sees to have been determined by local, tribal, or specific cultic custom—the Æsiric/Vanic distinction may have been key. In any event, with the coming of Christianity all cremation ceased, as did the practice of burying the dead with grave goods—objects they would need in the afterlife.

Whether the body is burned or buried, it is in either case literally decomposed. In the case of cremation, this is done rapidly by fire; in the case of inhumation, it occurs slowly by natural decay and consumption by subterranean creatures.

The essence of the mystery of *ear* is decay, or decomposition—a process if dissolution (*solve*) awaiting reconstitution on another level.

That this interpretation is both logical and historically supportable is suggested by the mythic importance of the cognate word in Old Norse—*aurr*. In the Alvíssmál (10) *aurr* is said to be the name of the earth among the *uppregin*—the "high gods." It is the substance which the Norns mix with the waters of the well of Urðr in order to nourish the cosmic tree, Yggdrasill, and keep it alive.[129] This substance—*aurr*—is the "fertilizer" for renewal, mixed with water which has been circulated to the top of the tree and which has fallen back down again into the well. *Aurr* is the substance of organic decay, but it provides new life if *used* properly.

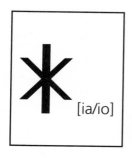

[ia/io]

OE *īar – īor*—meaning uncertain, perhaps a kind of fish, eel, newt, or serpent.

The meaning of this rune-name is fraught with controversy. The form of the word itself is not clear, nor is the description provided in the text of the OERP. This has led scholars to speculate widely.

In the OERP, ✳ is placed between ᴎ and ᛏ, although it is a later addition and belongs rather in the order we show here.

The OERP calls ✳ an *ēa-fix*, "river fish," but obviously it is no true fish, as the poem further states that it "enjoys its food on land." It is also said to have a "beautiful home surrounded by water." This also does not sound like a description of a fish.

Esoterically and symbolically, this rune is a reference to the serpent which makes its home in a grotto and which comes onto land to feed. The "food" the serpent craves may be the flesh of prey, but may also be the richness of gold. Fáfnir was described as having his lair near water.

A synthetic runologist, Karl Schneider, has offered an etymology of *ēor ~ īor* from a reconstructed PIE word **egwhris* > PGmc. *euriz*, "snake, worm." Cognates in other Indo-European languages include Sanskrit áhi and Avestan a¢i, "serpent." This etymology links *ēor* to the serpent.

The meaning of the serpent in Germanic lore is complex. There are the cosmic serpents Niðhöggr and Jörmungandr or the Miðgarðsormr ("Midgard's Serpent") as well as a number of dragons or wyrms (< OE *wyrm*, "serpent") in heroic mythology. In the case of *ēor*, we are dealing with a serpent of the

Jörmugnadr-type. It exists in the water and surrounds the world, holding the cosmos together in a restricting or limiting manner. The rune-shape ✳ is suggestive of this:

The world-tree pattern is basically one of a horizontal plane (shown by the earth and the four cardinal directions) and a central axis running through the middle—surrounded by the cosmic ocean. This pattern is also suggestive of a cosmic mill-work with the axis turning and driving the horizontal plane around.

[kw]

OE *cweorð*: "fire-bore."

Gothic letter-name quertra < Go. *qairþra, the name of the letter ᛩ [q, pronounced qu].

This word is only attested to as the rune-name for the [kw-] sound. The rune is variously shaped as ᛢ or ᛨ. Etymologically, the word is linked to PGmc. *kwernō, "mill-(stone)." The stem *kwer- indicates something which turns or spins or something which receives or takes something else in. The word may have existed in a masculine form *kwerþuz, "fire-bore," and a feminine one *kwerþrō, "fire bore-hole." This would then refer to the device by which the need-fire was generated using a vertical bore in a wooden socket which was filled with kindling.[130]

The theory that it is merely a rhyming nonsense word linked to the Old English name for the p-rune, *peorð*, does not seem plausible on typological grounds. All other rune-names are meaningful words; why would this be an exception?

Of all the rune-names, this one is the most difficult to understand logically because we have no poetic stanza to explain it and the word itself is otherwise unknown.

On an esoteric level, *cweorð* can be seen as a further refinement of the meaning of *nauðiz/nied*, and one that focuses on the receptacle of the fire, rather than the upper part of the need-fire apparatus. This socket in which the fire is actually produced is perhaps reflected in the shape of the Gothic letter: ᛩ .

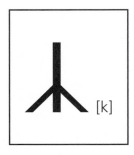

OE *calc ~ calic:* (< Lat. calix): "goblet, cup, chalice."

As a rune-name this word only occurs in the Old English tradition. It is clearly borrowing from the Latin, and therefore betrays an obvious Christian influence. The word is also known in Old Norse as *kalkr:* "chalice," which is taken from the Old English word. Old Norse *kalkr* can also be used in a pagan context,[131] whereas a related word, *kaleikr*, only occurs in ecclesiastical contexts.

The chalice in question is undoubtedly that used in the performance of the eucharistic ritual in the medieval church. This ritual would have been in principle one familiar to pagan Anglo-Saxons as the drinking of sacred liquids had also been a part of their heathen liturgy.

There is no poetic stanza ascribed to ᛣ, and the word is uniquely a borrowing from a non-Germanic language, but if we understand that this may well be an *interpretatio Christiana*, a Christian interpretation, of a pagan word and concept, a good deal of lore becomes clearer. The term it would have replaced is *horn*. Horns, most famously those belonging to the aurochs (ᛁᚢᛁ), were used as drinking vessels, both sacred and profane, by the Germanic peoples. The spectacular golden horns of Gallehus bear witness to just how important these were in religious practice and symbolism. Horns were even used in the early Germanic church in place of the Romano-Christian chalice—a practice outlawed by the church.

The word "horn" was even used as a sacred word formula on occasion.

In mythology, the receptacle or container of the sacred liquid—the poetic mead—was called Óðrœrir ("exciter of inspiration"). The individual horn of the participants in the ritualized drinking banquet practiced by the Germanic peoples—the symbel—would have been seen as a specific and particular manifestation of the great container of inspiration.

The final three runes of the thirty-three rune Fuþorc extension appear to have a special kinship, and this interpretation is pursued separately in appendix C of this book.

OE *stān:* "stone."
This does not occur as a rune-name elsewhere, but the rune itself may appear in one Frisian inscription, Westeremden B, (fifth to eighth century) in the form: ᛥ.

Here we have a name which is well-known in all Germanic languages, all derived from PGmc. *stainaz:* "stone." Obviously, the word "stone" appears often in runic inscriptions because the object upon which the inscription is made is so often mentioned. Among the oldest examples is the fragmentary stone of Vetteland (Norway, ca. 350), which identifies the object as "my son's stone" (. . . *magōR mīnas staina*).

In the absence of a poetic stanza to provide a basis for the lore intended to surround this rune, we are left to wonder as to its precise significance. The first thought that comes to mind is that it refers to the stones upon which runes are carved. In the runic tradition, the stone itself signified the principle of eternity, the eternity into which the message of the inscription was cast, or "set in stone." The principle of *stān* is eternity and permanence.

Stones were used as altars by the ancient Germanic peoples, and standing stones were erected as memorials and grave markers even before the advent of runic writing.

The stone being referenced in the Anglo-Frisian Fuþorc may be a special and particular stone implied by the runic context of *calc* and *gār*. For more on this possibility, see appendix C.

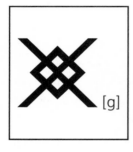

OE *gār:* "spear, javelin, dart."
This word is a common Germanic term for a spear, e.g., **ON** *geirr:* spear," **OHG** *keir:* spear." This appears to be a word shared from antiquity with Italic, e.g., **Lat**. *gaesum.* See also **O.Ir**. *gaē:* "spear."

All we have to go on as far as the significance of this rune is concerned is the name, meaning, and the rich mythic and cultural context for the object the name denotes.

In the military culture of the Germanic peoples, the spear was an essential weapon. It was used as a projectile, but more often as a thrusting and slashing weapon. Bronze Age rock carvings and early Germanic art feature the spear prominently, as shown on page 141.

The general principle of *gār* is the extension of power. The spear extends power beyond the personal sphere and projects it to a target. The PGmc. form of the word is *gaizaz*. It is reflected in a number of Indo-European languages, e.g., O.Ir. *gaé*, "spear," and as a loanword in Greek χαιος, "shepherd's stick." This latter association is significant because the image of Wōðanaz in a wide-brimmed hat carrying a spear and that of the wide-brimmed (shepherd's) hat worn by the Greek god Hermes who also carries a long stick (his shepherd's staff) show archaic iconographic connections. The word would appear to have originally been a Celto-Germanic term, in the same way the word *rūnō* is shared between them.

In myth, the spear plays several important roles. It is the symbolic weapon and royal scepter of the god Wōðanaz. It is used to kill sacrificial victims as they hang in trees—as the god was so wounded in the tree Yggdrasill (Hávamál 138–39). It is used as a magico-operative tool with which to dedicate an opposing army to die in battle as human sacrifices to the god Wōðanaz or Teiwaz.

In the world of ancient Germanic legal and political ritual, the spear played a central role. A young man would receive a spear when he was initiated into the clan as a free and full-grown man with the right to bear arms. This spear would be carried in legal assemblies, and it is by movements of the spear that votes were taken in the assembly, or thing. This practice is responsible for the origin of the name Shakespeare.

The spear was the Germanic scepter—a symbol of the chieftain's authority—but it was also a sign of the clan or tribe itself in its organic solidarity and link with its divine ancestors. There are several spearheads from the archeological record which give evidence of these beliefs. Some have abstract symbols and runes inscribed on them. These are discussed in some detail in the book *Mysteries of the Goths*.[132]

The spear or gar is a symbol of a man's full power in a legal sense, which links him with the gods by symbolic analogy.

In the operative record of the ancient Germanic peoples, we find an example of how the spear was used in the form of the shaft of a throwing spear from Kragehul, Denmark, 525 CE. The (normalized) inscription appears:

ᛖᚲᛖᚱᛁᛚᚨ ᚤᚱᛊᚢᚷᛁᛖᛚᛖ ᛊᛗᚢᚾᚨᚾᚨᛁᛏᛖ ᚷᚷᚷᚷ ᛁᚻᚢᚷᚻᛖ
ᛚᚨᚠ ᚾᚨᚷᚨᛚᛚᛁᚨᚢᛒᛁᚷ

Which translates to:

I, the Erulian, am called Ásgísl's retainer (or "son")—
ᚷᚷᚷ—magically-working ᚷ. To helm-destroying hail I consecrate by means of the spear . . .

The bind-rune g has been interpreted as either the phrase *gibu auja*, "I give good luck" or perhaps more conservatively, "given [i.e., consecrated] to the god (*ansuz*)!" This latter interpretation would bring the formula in line with the passage in the Hávamál (stanza 138): *geiri undaðr ok gefinn Óðni*—"wounded by spear and give to Odin. . ." This spear shaft of Kragehul is also a direct corroboration of the ritual hurling of a spear as a magico-religious act preceding battle mentioned in the Völuspá (stanza 24). The bind-rune could also simply mean: "I give (the opposing army) to the god."

CHAPTER THREE

A THEORY OF OPERATIVE RUNOLOGY

The perennial problem with regard to runes and magic is the exact theory by which the systems of the foregoing stave-lore were used in antiquity to effect changes in the human environment. In one of my roles in life—that of an academic runologist—I may be accused of being "unscientific" because of my explorations of Germanic spirituality and operative runology. That such an accusation would never be made against a practicing Roman Catholic who dared to write about the history of the medieval church in an academic venue speaks to the hypocrisy of the accusation. The Catholic would on the contrary be extolled for having "special insight" into the matters under discussion, whereas one who writes of the myths of Odin must have no spiritual or intellectual connections to these myths—to have such affinities would put "objectivity" at risk.

In point of fact, the German philosopher Friedrich Schleiermacher (1768–1834) established that in order to interpret a spiritual or religious system *accurately* one *must have* an empathetic link with it. How can something so much a part of the subjective universe of humanity, such as a myth represents, be entirely *objectified*, made separate from the inner world of the interpreter, and at the same time have any hope of true understanding emerge from this process? Obviously it could not. From the academic perspective my delvings into the subjective universe of the ancient runemasters can be viewed as experimental paleology—experiential trials in the assumption of thought modalities retrieved from literature, archeology, runology, and folklore (seasoned with comparative evidence from organically related traditions). This process is akin to that undertaken by experimental archeologists who attempt to recreate artifacts using the same technologies as the ancients. We attempt to reawaken thought forms using our intellectual and spiritual capacities.

Here I will present a comprehensive theory of operative runology which represents a synthesis of the best academic, or scientific, theories of magic and practical theories of magic. This synthesis of science and spiritual practice has a long heritage among runologists—the first being the father of modern runology, Johannes Bureus.

Both the scientific and spiritual worlds will have something to learn from this process. I would like to emphasize at this point that the current practice of runic spirituality may provide an insight here or there for understanding obscure practices reflected in runic inscriptions, but that these contemporary practices do not reflect exact practices from antiquity. Current practice is inspired by models from the past, but they are separate things—between which there remains a certain resonance. The world of Egill is not my world, and so my magic cannot be his magic.

The Scientific Theory of Rune-Magic

Over the course of my career, I have addressed the topic of an academic or scientific theory of how rune-magic works on more than one occasion.[133] In what follows one will find material from these various texts explaining magic from an academically acceptable perspective. This is valuable because today academics are more likely to ask the question: "How does magic work?" in a less judgmental way than they have in the past when magic was ascribed to "erroneous thinking."

Several theories of magic have been forwarded in the ethnological literature over the years. These are too disparate to be delineated in their entirety here. Our purpose is to present an overview of some major concepts and to synthesize them into a view consistent with the latest academic theories on the topic, theories which we will later be able to apply in practical ways.

The first theoretical synthesis of the study of magic was given by Sir James Frazer.[134] Although his overall view of magic as a form of "erroneous thought" and product of primitive man's lack of knowledge concerning causal relationships, and his *evolutionary* model in which he saw "magic" as the first stage in a development in which the second stage is "religion," and the third stage is "science" has been generally rejected, his ideas concerning the sympathetic basis for operative thinking have fallen on more fertile ground.

In magical theory, the law of sympathy states that "like attracts like." It presupposes a hidden link between things, and most especially between concrete *things* and *symbols* of them—both of which are seen as being one in the magical universe. Therefore, it is thought that through the manipulation of a *symbol*, its corresponding *object* may be similarly manipulated.

Various "power concepts" are also important to magical theories. These have historically been seen to fall into two categories: 1) the dynamistic and 2) the animistic. This dichotomy, although perhaps an oversimplification, does seem to have solid foundations in the magical models of traditional peoples. The dynamistic corresponds to that magical power which is manipulated, gathered, and dispensed as if it were a concrete force of nature—almost as a type of "electricity." This dynamistic force is perhaps best known by the Polynesian word *mana*. In the Norse world this is exemplified by *hamingja*. The basic concept remains one which is essentially *impersonal*.

On the other hand, animism lends itself to a more personalized conceptualization. A belief in psychoid beings—which may be seen as great gods or goddesses, or as lesser divinities, or very commonly as ancestral spirits—is often an important aspect of magico-religious worldviews. Both dynamism and animism are involved with the idea that "everything is alive," but dynamistic force is a relatively rare thing—possessed by certain objects, persons, or even numinous (animistic) beings themselves—and not by others. But animistic thinking posits that everything has a life somewhat akin to human or animal life, or that the mode of dealing with such psychoid entities is akin to dealings with living things. Rocks, streams, and trees have "spirits"—all of which may be manipulated if the proper procedures are carried out by the proper person.[135] Within an animistic model it is possible that the "spirit" will resist efforts to manipulate it or refuse attempts to communicate with it. This is not possible with a dynamistic model, however, and so the burden of the correct performance and use of proper materials become even more important. Both dynamism and animism seem to coexist as magical views among most peoples, and in fact, they appear to complement one another.

Besides the "law of sympathy" and these two concepts of magical power, another pivotal aspect is that of the human will or consciousness. Here it is essential to remember that among the Germanic peoples the human being is thought to be composed of what might best be described as a psychosomatic complex. Certain elements of such a complex could give special personas active access to both dynamistic and animistic concepts of power. In all cases the primary element would be that of the *will*, the faculty of desire, which is the motivating agent in any magical operation.

A kind of "missing link," which seems to have been implicit in models of magic all along, but which has only been explicitly formulated since the late 1960s, might best be described as the semiotic theory or model.[136] Basic to this theory is the idea of *communication*, and the model is most clearly understood as a metalinguistic one.[137]

Basic to all forms of communication is that there is a sender and a receiver of messages. In order to send a message, it must be encoded into a system which will be intelligible to the receiver, then put into a medium which becomes the instrument of the transmission. Once the transmission has been received by the receiver, it can then respond in one way or another.

Fundamental to the work of van Baal is man's ability to effect communication with his universe and to "think ascriptively," i.e., hidden meaning is *ascribed* to the phenomena of the universe and it becomes a virtual partner in this form of communication. Such a model of communication implies the real existence of two subjects, or "doers" of action: 1) man and 2) the hidden other side of the universe.[138] The "other side" is the recipient of man's magical message, and in turn, it becomes the active agent of an action of which man becomes the recipient.

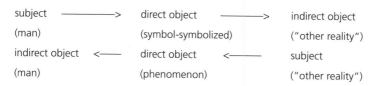

In his analysis of the nature of a magical spell, van Baal summarizes his ideas on this communicative relationship:

The formula takes its origin from the discourse between man and his universe, in the case of a particular formula a discourse concerning a certain object and the fulfillment of a desire. In this discourse man feels addressed or singled out by his universe, and he endeavors to address it in turn, trying to discover the kind of address to which his universe will be willing to answer, that is, willing to show itself communicable. The formula he finally discovers in answer to his quest is not really man's discovery but a gift, a revelation bestowed upon him by his universe. The formula is the outcome of an act of communication in which man's universe reveals to him the secret of how it should be addressed in this or that circumstance, a secret which is at the same time a revelation of its hidden essence in that particular field.[139]

Van Baal's views emphasize a causal function within the "hidden other reality," with which man communicates with his equally real volition, and from which he receives responses in the form of phenomena.

The strict cause/effect model is somewhat called into question with the new emphasis on the idea of "analogical thinking" in the magical model proposed by Tambiah (1968; 1973) and Finnegan (1969). For both Tambiah and Finnegan, the ideas drawn from Austin (1962) on "performative speech," are fundamental: ". . . ritual acts and magical rites are the 'illocutionary' (see Austin 1962: 98ff. on 'illocution') or 'performative' sort, which simply by virtue of being enacted (under appropriate conditions) achieve a change of state or do something effective. . . ."[140] For Tambiah, magical acts are "'performative' acts by which a property is imperatively transferred to a recipient object or person on an analogical basis.".[141] The idea of magical analogy could quite easily be understood in terms of what Frazer and others called "sympathy." However, "analogy" has the advantage of being in the context of this more comprehensive "linguistic model" of magical theory. In the model posited by Tambiah, the idea of *appropriateness* within an entire "frame of reference" (much as Grambo [1975] understands it) is the basis for magical effectiveness, and thereby the mechanistic cause/effect model is ameliorated.

A semiotic model, in which magic is seen as a *message*, is discussed by Grambo (1975). This study is especially valuable because the author makes use of historical Scandinavian sources and advocates a restriction of magical definitions to limited cultural areas. According to Grambo,[142] the first step in understanding how a magical act works is the comprehension of the "frame of reference" in which the act takes place. This is of both an objective (environmental) and subjective (psychological) category, and Grambo further analyzes the factors as 1) the social group to which one belongs, 2) the private experiences of each individual, 3) the psychological condition of each individual, and 4) the gender of the individual. This "frame" would then seem to act as a matrix, a kind of underlying meta-semantics or grammar in which magical messages are encoded. The magician then uses this code to transmit the magical message. Grambo's model appears:

Frame of Reference

transmitter	message	recipient
(magician)	(magic)	(human victim, supernatural being, object, etc.)

A further element of the semiotic model is that of magical symbols and symbol systems. In magical operations, these symbol systems are complex. In function, however, they all share two fundamental aspects: 1) magico-analogous unity with the object of the symbol, and 2) the symbol is capable of manipulation through the agency of the human will. Whole systems of these symbols could then constitute a sort of magical lexicon, and this, within the psycho-cultural frame of reference, composes the semantics of magic over which the trained magician has at least partial command. The exact ontological relationship between the symbol and the thing symbolized remains ambiguous, but essentially it would appear to oscillate on a continuum between the two poles of 1) symbol/numinous object identity, and 2) the independent existence of the symbol in its own right which might possess the power to attract or repel a secondary numinous force or being. Thus we have both a *direct*, and an *indirect* mode of operative (= magical) symbolic communication. The magician either acts *as* a god to make things happen, or he communicates to a god to *have* something done for him.

A synthetic view of the semiotic theory of magic might be summarized as follows: By means of willed performative or operative acts/speech, the operator/magician (subject) is able to manipulate, or to participate in, a complex of symbols which have an analogical ("sympathetic") connection to the indirect object of these acts. Because the psycho-cosmological and social frame of reference for such operative acts ascribes a grammatically subjective nature to this indirect object of the action, it is considered a partner in a phenomenologically communicative process, and it in turn becomes the subject/agent of an action of which the magician or some other person(s) or thing(s) become the object.

The articulation of a comprehensive theory, or even complete definition of "magic," from a scientific perspective is a daunting task. From the most recent scientific work done in the field of magico-religious theory, it is clear that the process variously known as "symbolist," "operative," "instrumental," or "semiotic," in which the magician, by means of symbols, is able to communicate with a wider reality (of which he himself is also an integral part), provides the best general theory for examining traditions such as the runes. Complexities arise when this process is seen within the holistic context or frame of reference (which would include components we could call "social," "psychological," "cosmological," "theological," etc.), which give it its potency. This process may be conceptualized as a mode of operative communication with a "causal reality" which utilizes the whole environment. As far as a working scientific definition of "magic" is concerned, I would suggest: a technique by which the human being is able, by the power of volition expressed though symbols, to influence events in subjective and/or objective reality.

As can be seen from the foregoing discussion, which has been adapted from the more extensive text of the book *Runes and Magic* (Rûna-Raven, 2010), the academic theories of magic have much to teach the would-be practitioner of magical operations. These are no sterile theories, but rather dynamic concepts full of useful ideas for the current operative runologist.

The Traditional Theory of Rune-Magic

The ancient runemasters from the Viking Age, such as Egill Skallagrímsson, or from the Migration Age, such as the Erulian who carved the stone of Järsberg, all operated on a theory of rune-magic. All practicing magicians have theories by which they operate, so they would have been no different. However, no explanatory treatise ever appeared in ancient times explaining this theory in their own words. They had no need of such conscious theorizing, because the culture in which they lived was so highly contextual—most things were organically connected to one another—which is typical of traditional cultures in general. The underlying theory, like almost all ancient and traditional theories of magic, must be reconstructed or reverse engineered, from the evidence that is left to us.

For the ancients it was self-evident that the runes had first been received by a god, Wōðanaz/Óðinn, and that they formed an encoded link between the cosmos and this god—the model of consciousness made manifest. It was equally self-evident that those who knew these runes (secrets) and could write them must have a direct traditional link to the god who first received them. With the runes the universe could be read (divination), and the runes could be used to communicate actively and directly with the cosmos and the gods through writing, or carving, the runes. Therefore, it can be said that traditionally the runes are the code for communication with the gods and with the world, whereby events, phenomena, knowledge, and nature itself can be both understood and shaped. The runic code provides a key for the interpretation of events or phenomena and omens or signs (ON *heill*, OE *hwatu*) from the gods. Runes likewise offer an operative table of semiotic characters by which events or phenomena can be *written* into reality. This is basically the straightforward way in which Egill or the runemaster of Noleby would have understood how the runes *worked*. Additionally, of course, they would have understood that the operator or reader must possess a nature or character which is "in tune" with the gods—it not only matters *what* is done, but *who* is doing it. This separates operative runology from any sort of "science."

Theory of Radical Operative Runology

Radical runology is a kind of understanding of the runes that takes all of the fundamentals relating to the runes—scientific and traditional—into account. This approach synthesizes the rationally, historically based data and analysis on one side and the mythic and traditional approach on the other. Whereas the historical record is best understood after being submitted to the scientific method, the traditional aspect is best described as an art form. Radical runology is therefore a synthesis of science and art. Its form is unlikely to satisfy strict adherents of either extreme of this spectrum of human endeavor—but it is our contention that the earliest practice of runology emerged from just such an *ur*-synthesis, or root, and that in the final analysis purely scientific methodologies, although they have much of value to teach, cannot reconstruct the level of understanding necessary to unlock the runic secrets. By the same token, overly subjective and speculative approaches, unanchored in the historical record and actual runic data, are even less likely to help us understand anything of value.

ELEMENTS OF RADICAL OPERATIVE RUNOLOGY

Radical operative runology is a system of meta-communication. In principle, radical operative runology consists of four elements or theoretical components: 1) similarity of systems, 2) common encoder, 3) frame of reference, and 4) discovery of the event horizon. The art and science of mastering these elements, and most importantly becoming the kind of human being who is capable of mastering them, are the secret.

Similarity of Systems: We have learned in connection with theories of communication in general that those systems, e.g., beings, machines, which are *most similar* to one another will communicate *best* with one another. People can communicate with dogs, but two dogs communicate more perfectly with one another than any person can hope to. In magic and religion we first look to systems of gods (:ᚨ:) and men (:ᛗ:). Myth tells us why and how men possess a systemic similarity to the gods—the gifting of spiritual and even aesthetic components by Wōðanaz-Wiljōn-Wīhaz (see Völuspá 17–18 and Gylfaginning 13). Judeo-Christian tradition leaves us with a vague notion of man being created "in god's image," but Eddic sources tell us many more details. Men and gods have approximately similar spiritual or psychic components—but they are not absolutely identical. Men are not gods—or at least the vast majority are not. The more similar a man can be to a god, the better he will be able to do works similar to those of the gods—the better he can "hear" their voices, "speak" to them, and undertake workings with relation to the wider cosmos similar to their own. Therefore the first and greatest work of magic is initiation—development of the self to become increasingly godlike. This process takes place on two levels: energy and essence. An inner enthusiasm for things divine must be cultivated, and one's character must be refined to be more analogous to the divine as well. This does not equate to milksop and moralistic clichés of Judeo-Christian notions of the "divine" in man. Our exemplary models are Óðinn and Freyja!

$$ᚠ + ᛗ = ᛗᚠ$$

In any event magic, our operative runology, can only be success-fully attempted by *certain* individuals and then only imperfectly. Men are not gods.

How and why humans interact with gods through a reso-nance of being have their roots in the gifts of the gods—which include divine consciousness. That this gift exists objectively is proven by the fact that humans function in ways different from other animals. (This is not to say that certain other animals do not possess an element of the divine consciousness, it is just that they are limited in what kind they manifest, whereas humans are free to manifest anything they can.) This difference must have an origin and a cause: this we call the triad—Wōðanaz-Wiljōn-Wīhaz. Humans possess a quality which exists in a dimension beyond time and space as we know them which can objectively be referred to as the *hyperbody*. Just as a geometri-cal figure, such as the cube, may be seen to possess a hyper-state, a hypercube,[143] beyond its three-dimensional existence, so too does the human being possess a hyperbody. The hypercube can be imagined but not seen or represented in the realm of Midgard, i.e., the world of five senses and three dimensions. But the hyperbody exists for humans, just as surely as the hypercube or tesseract exists. It is with this "body" that we resonate with the unmanifest, divine realm.

Common Encoder: The encoder, as we learned when discussing the scientific theory of operative runology, is the system of devices by which an operative communication is formulated. The encoder is the language of communication. This encoder must be shared by the sender (magician) and receiver (god or universe). The possibility of successful communication implies the presence of this encoder/decoder in common between sender and receiver. This is the secret behind the so-called magical link phenomenon. Traditionally, this commonality of the encoder is attributed to the spiritual gifts given to humankind by the gods, coupled with a more specific transfer of runic knowledge from Óðinn to the first runemaster, who then selectively taught this knowledge among mankind.

The entirety of the runic code is greater than just knowledge of the sound values attributed to each stave. There are many "encoding elements" present in the process of runic operations. First is, of course, the correct use of the runestaves to represent sound. Other elements include the choice of substance upon which an inscriptions is made—stone, bone, metal, wood—and the placement of the object, e.g., within a sacred space or in a place of high prestige or visibility for many people. Additional elements are hiding or sending. Runes can be hidden both physically (e.g., burying the inscription or concealing it in some other way) and by means of rune-codes or bind-runes. This latter manner conceals the content and meaning in plain sight. The idea of concealment is an extension of the runic principle itself. The mystery is something unknown or unknowable. By imitating this quality, the communication is *meta-poetically* brought into closer harmony with the realm of the divine (also mysterious) and thus rendered more effective. Another important corollary to hiding is the act of *sending*. Messages are usually sent in one fashion or another. The two most prevalent modes of sending are burning and burying. When a message is burnt, it is sent quickly *upward* to the heavenly region; when it is buried, it is sent *downward* to the chthonic region. Neither of these regions or techniques refer to anything "good" or "evil"; gods and goddesses, as well as nature, exist above as well as below. Messages are also commonly submerged in water or bogs. Each of these modes of transmission must be chosen to be in accord with the meaning and intent of the message. In all of this, it becomes increasingly clear just how much operative runology is an *art* as much as it is a science.

Frame of Reference: Another way of expressing this idea would be "cultural context." For an operation to work, it must act within a frame of reference. Our major endeavor in current operative runology is to restore our lost frame of reference, which will in turn cause our operations to be better. Our ancestors lived in a culture with a *high level* of cultural context—they spoke a Germanic language, worshipped Germanic gods, and were surrounded by material and intellectual features consistent with the Germanic aesthetic sense and sensibility. We, on the other hand, live in a society with a relatively *low level* of cultural context. We speak a Germanic language, but one that has been hybridized with French, Latin, and Greek elements; the majority of the people worship a foreign god; and our aesthetic universe is eclectic, if not chaotic, in the extreme.

When it comes to the frame of reference, the operative runologist has three tasks and choices ahead—discovering it, accepting it, and transforming it. These are three very different tasks. To discover the frame of reference or cultural context in which you live is a formidable, and often depressing, endeavor. You have to see the "world" for what it *is*, not what you wish it *were*. Having discovered it, you must at least provisionally, and for the sake of effective magical operations, *accept it* for what it is. You have to work within this world as it presently exists. This is the doctrine of *magical pragmatism*. But it may be your task, as it has become mine, to transform the cultural context—to return it to its timeless patterns and values. The greatest acts of magic involve turning the frame of reference in a willful way. This third aspect is not necessary to the ability to perform sorcery, but it is heroic. Those who attempt it are most remembered in history.

Because we do not share the exact cultural context as our ancestors, we cannot reproduce the exact magical effects of ancient runemasters. They lived in a high context semiotic environment, and ours is extremely low context. Much of the concerted effort of advanced operative runology today is focused on the recovery of context—personally and transpersonally.

The Event Horizon: The event horizon is that liminal space whence phenomena enter the world from an unmanifested state. The unmanifest becomes manifest. Operations of magic can be conducted entirely within the manifest universe; physical signs are used to evoke physical responses. All advertising or political propaganda works on this level. However, another form of operation causes changes in the pre- or unmanifest world—before this phenomenological feed enters the physical realm. To communicate with this unmanifest—or runic—realm requires the highest form of art and science—and often times luck. But this is where the most miraculous changes can be effected. This operation requires a form of time-travel—because it is from the realm of the "past" (*Urðr*) whence these phenomena arise in our lives—he who learns to condition the past can control the future.

Man and the Tree

One of the key components of a radical theory of operative runology is the ancient Germanic doctrine of psycho-cosmology. What is psycho-cosmology? It is the teaching that humankind was specifically said to have been shaped from *trees* (ash and elm) by the gods, and that the cosmos itself is also said to have an arboreal form. The ancient sages are telling us that there is some metaphorical secret shared between the essences of what a tree is and what the world and mankind are. The tree forms another connecting link between the mind of the magician and events in the world. The key to accessing this flow of information is to realize—to make real—the fullness of the tree within the individual's hyperbody (or psyche). Then those parts of the hyperbody which correspond to parts in the cosmos—or more correctly actually resonate with them—can be stimulated to cause changes in the outer world. Once this state is achieved, the absolute distinctions between god-man-world can be momentarily dissolved—at which time the individual can act directly on the universe itself. Such states of being are always temporary and fleeting—but it is in these moments that magic occurs.

A DEFINITION OF OPERATIVE RUNOLOGY

The overriding fact about the runes is that they are symbols for communication. Secondarily, the best and at once most scientific, and most elegantly artful, definition or theory of magic makes it abundantly clear that magic is dependent upon a system of *communication* between the individual will of the magician and the elements of the universe which lie outside of, or apart from, the individual will. In the runes our ancient ancestors found a universal encoder and decoder for effecting communication between the individual mind and the rest of the world. Runic communication is a conversation with the universe in which messages are sent, received by the target of this transmission—be it god or the fabric of the world itself— and then responded to in a way which resonates with the character of the original transmission. The universe constantly "communicates" with the individual through the five senses, but also by what *happens* to the individual. We experience events or phenomena as received messages from the world. By modifying the transmission by means of the universal encoder—the runes—we may modify what happens.

CHAPTER FOUR

THE PRACTICE OF OPERATIVE RUNOLOGY

It is now time to put the theories of operative runology into practice. This is the art and practice of doing things with runes—accomplishing willed ends by means of mysteries. Nothing can be more enigmatic and at the same time precisely defined as this. What the world calls "rune-magic" is in essence the art and science of utilizing the ancient Germanic symbol system known as "runes" in a process of meta-communication between the magician and the world around him. We shall now learn how to use the runes in this process.

How to Do Things with Runes

In ancient times runes were primarily used to represent natural language—but it was embodied in a form and character unlike the spoken word. It was more permanent and made speech visible, rather than just heard. These facts made runes highly suited to the purposes of *magic*. Cultic speech is a feature of Indo-European linguistic culture. The written form could destroy or deform the sanctity of this speech if it was not synthesized with the dominant esoteric culture of the time. This was apparently done from the beginning, and this is why the runes have so many features that go beyond the necessities of merely representing spoken sounds. From the beginning, or from early on, runes were used in three communicative modalities which went beyond natural speech and entered the realm of *operation*— doing things with words.

THE THREE MODALITIES

These three modalities, or ways of operation, are:

1) Isolate

2) Contextual

3) Synthetic

That is, runes can be expressions of their isolated name/symbolic value; they can be strung together to create representations of the spoken word and convey two-level communications as a combination of perfected visible speech made up of individual symbols; and they can be forged or welded together to create combinations of meaning.

The *isolate rune* has a symbolic meaning unto itself. We know that in ancient times individual runes were used in texts to represent the word which was the traditional *name* of the rune. For example, ᛟ stands for Old English *ēþel*, meaning "homeland," in written records. Therefore, any and all individual runes can always be understood to represent the symbolic quality of their names, and thus even words can be interpreted as formulas made up of these qualities. The word *alu* means "drink of magical inspiration" on one level, but it can also be seen as a formula made up of *ansuz-laguz-uruz*: "god-liquid-power." In the ancient operative inscriptions, we see an example of this usage in the Gummarp stone, where three f-runes are appended to the inscription = *fehu* × 3.

Contextual runes take the individual staves and linearly string them together into words which make sense on a natural level. Transcendent principles in the runes are arranged in a manner which renders a mundane meaning—thus the heavenly is made terrestrial. There is great poetic, and hence magical, meaning in this process. Ancient runemasters prized the ability to create multileveled communications. This idea of placing many layers of meaning into a creation is very common in the ancient and medieval worlds. A runic message which makes sense on a natural as well as a transcendental level is the height of the runic art. Remember that it is best to use English runes for modern English compositions of this sort—reserving the younger and older runes for communications composed in Old Norse and Proto-Germanic, respectively. The major principle at work here is that the natural meaning of the language "fine-tunes" the message, while its execution in runes begins the process of *sending* it into a realm where the message can begin to take effect. When the pagan runemaster carved ᚾᛏᚱᚦᛁ + ᛏᛏ + ᚱᛏᛏᛏ + ᛏᚾᛑ + ᛏᛏ + ᛏᚱᛑᛉᛁ + ᛑᚾᛏᚢ + ᚺᛁᚱ + ᛁᛏᚺ + ᛉᛏᚢᛑᚾᛁ + ᛑᚱᚢᚺ: "May the one become a **rati** and a perverse woman who carves a cross (on this stone)." The master states what will happen if the stone is violated—but it is done in runes which makes the natural statement or "wish" into a phenomenological reality. Words become events.

Synthetic runes are those which are bound or blended together to form a runic compound. This is technically effected by means of bind-runes. In ancient times this began as a combining of runes which were adjacent to one another in a text: *ek* ᛖᚲ becomes *ék* ᛗ = "I." This was done in order to save space, manipulate the rune-count (two runes brought together to count as only one), create abbreviations for sacred formulas, or meld the meanings of the two runes.[144] But eventually this idea developed into an independent art form, and magical staves (Ice. *galdrastafir*) began to be formulated from complex runic combinations.[145]

These three modalities of working with runes provide a wide range of communicative and aesthetic possibilities. The advanced runer is able to craft very precise communications with the realm of causality by using these methods. However, the magic is not entirely within the *objects*—or the science—but rather it mostly resides in the *subject*—the runer.

Foundations of Practice

People who think magic works like science are mistaken. Those who believe magic has objective rules that, if followed correctly, will yield the prescribed results are in error. The chief reason these statements are true is that magic and its operation hinge mainly on the state of being of the operator—the magician himself. This state of being has two aspects: capacity and performance. One can only perform within one's capacity, and this capacity is subject to development. But each individual performance will vary in its level of power, and thus efficacy. This is true of every human endeavor. Magic is no different.

The operative runologist must first and foremost be dedicated to the development of the self—of the very capacity or ability to do magic. This development consists of three components, the internalization of three things: staves, myths, and culture. The meanings and very living essence of each of the runestaves must be absorbed into one's very being. The myths and the mythic world which they define and which defines them must likewise be synthesized into one's being. Finally, the general underlying cultural principles which eternally give shape to our mysteries must be understood and absorbed. This is a process which requires time and considerable effort. But without it operative runology is difficult to effect.

This process is described and outlined in the text of the book *The Nine Doors of Midgard* (Rûna-Raven, 2004, 3rd ed.), which must be considered a prerequisite for the practice of advanced operative runology.

To summarize the process: One meditates on each individual rune for a long time. In conjunction with this, one reads and enacts internally the mythic structures contained in the *Eddas*, the *Völsunga Saga*, and *Beowulf*. The internalized data is regularly measured against one's own experience in contemporary culture and reflected upon in the context of the long history of our culture. Once the runes are planted and cultivated in this way, they will begin to come alive within you, and you will be ready to *operate*.

Frame Workings

It is generally the case that acts of magic in which any sort of ritual is involved have formalized beginnings and endings. This conforms to the basic structure of transformational acts, in which there is a rite of separation from the profane or ordinary world, followed by the transformational act itself, and the whole is then concluded by an act of reintegration, or reentry, into the profane world. This idea of a formal beginning and ending creates a space in time within which the operation is focused or concentrated. If nothing else, this is a valuable tool for directing the will of the magician, blocking out external distractions, and so on.

Some schools of magic, especially those stemming from the Middle East, emphasize the concept that the beginning of a ritual should focus on *banishing* evil influences and *protecting* the magician from potentially malevolent forces. The Germanic tradition does not emphasize this aspect. Rather, the desired effects come about naturally as a result of the process of hallowing the place of working.

Hallowing takes place in two forms. In the ancient Germanic languages there were two terms for the "holy" (*wīhaz* and *hailagaz*) and similarly two verbs for "to make holy" (*wīhjanan* and *hailagōjanan*). The stem *wīh-* indicates something "set apart"—that is, separated from the ordinary or profane. Whereas the stem *hail-* signifies something "filled with the power of health or well-being." To our ancient ancestors, these were the two ways to hallow or sanctify a time or place: 1) set it apart, and 2) fill it with power. This process is conceptually seen in this diagram:

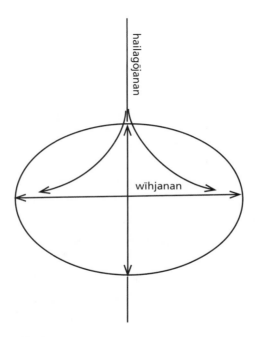

We have direct runic evidence that staves were sanctified by divine power in the formula: *Þórr wigi þessar rúnar*, which we see in inscriptions from Viking Age Denmark.[146]

The ritual space/time must be hallowed—set apart and filled with sacred power—so that the ritual or operation can proceed. These external symbols are, in fact, ways of expressing the deeper reality that the magician him- or herself must *rise up* into a special state of being and be filled with divine power before a successful operation can be completed.

BEGINNING WORKING

To open a ritual, it is useful to have a set piece of work which begins to create the conditions of separation and effusion with power. This is really all that is important. However you do this is acceptable, but we will offer some concrete suggestions as to how this can be done in a traditional manner.

Those who have studied my previous books, for example, *Futhark* or *The Nine Doors of Midgard*, will be familiar with such workings as the Hammer Rite or the *Elhaz* Rite.[147] These remain useful tools. However, it must be emphasized that they are rites for the temporary erection of sacred time/space. It is preferable to have permanent holy steads—places that are perpetually sacred and that when entered automatically transform the operator into a sacred state. Most people will not be able to afford such places, so we will offer more pragmatic and traditional methods of creating temporary working space/time.

AN OPENING WORKING

Gather the instruments of your working and place them in a spot convenient for your use. Sit or stand in the center of the space you wish to hallow and in which you wish to work. Visualize a square around you—this should be walls of transcendent energy. Within this square visualize the walls of a triangle as shown in diagram 1. Along the walls are inscribed the runes arranged in the three *ættir*, either of the Younger Fuþark or the Older Fuþark. If you use the Old English Fuþorc, the first twenty-four runes are visualized along the walls of the triangle, but you hold a staff carved with the other nine runes. The runes begin with ᚠ on the right in the angle in the north, as shown in diagram 2 on page 170.

Now cause your consciousness to enter into the geometrical forms surrounding you—first enter the square in the middle of the northern wall and move your mind through it as shown by

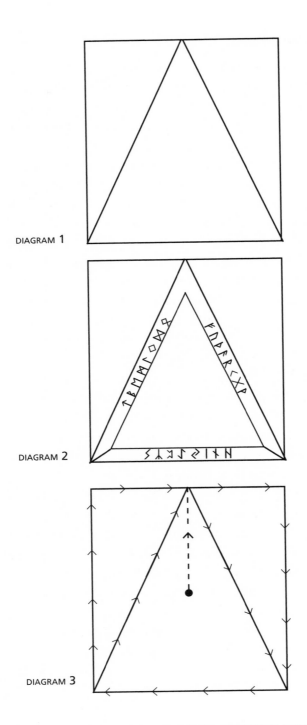

DIAGRAM 1

DIAGRAM 2

DIAGRAM 3

the arrows in diagram 3. Focus your mind on the feeling of the utter *separation* of this space from the world around it. Once this circuit is complete, stop and feel this state of sacrality. Now enter the triangle and move along with the runes, you may now recite their names—as your mind moves through the triangle and the *ættir* of runes, focus on how they fill the space with a power from beyond. As you conclude this, raise your arms in the ᛦ-rune gesture or posture. The aim of the working is to create a temporary sacred space and fill that space with the potential of runic energy and meaning. Seal the working with the words:

> So long as I will, this time and stead are warded against the outside, so long as I will, this time and stead are filled with the might and main of the gods, making this work—*wīh-hailag*!

ANOTHER OPENING WORKING

Especially if you work with Old Norse and Icelandic magical forms, this working is an ideal one for establishing a secure working stead. It can, however, be modified for other magical idioms. Iceland is said to be surrounded and protected by four "land spirits" (Ice. *landvættir*). These are even depicted on several modern Icelandic coins. First described in the *Heimskringla* of Snorri Sturluson, these entities are said to render Iceland invulnerable to invasion.[148] The saga tells of a sorcerer (*kunnigr maðr*) is sent by King Harald Gormsson of Denmark to do reconnaissance to see if the island could be invaded. The sorcerer goes out in the shape of a whale, and as he moves around the island, he sees these four *landvættir* guarding the land: a dragon in the east, a large bird in the north, a bull in the west, and a mountain giant (*bergrisi*) with an iron bar in his hand in the south. The sorcerer returns to Denmark and reports that it would not be feasible to attack Iceland because it was well-protected by its land wights.

Such *landvættir* were at one point commonly believed to have inhabited all Germanic lands. This idea is further evidenced by the fact that the serpent or dragon heads commonly used on Viking ships were intended to drive off the *landvættir* of countries being raided. This was why Icelandic law was later to mandate that the dragon heads had to be removed from the ships when they approached Iceland itself.[149]

A Call to the Landvættir

Stand in the middle of the space you intend to sanctify.

Face east and with arms uplifted in the Y-rune posture, say:

From the East swims the dragon, to the dread of my foes.

Then turn to the north and in the same posture say:

From the North flies the earn, to give me insight.

Next, turn to the west and say:

From the West charges the bull, to give me might and main.

And finally turn to the south and speak the formula:

From the South strides forth the rock giant, to make me steadfast.

As you do each of these stations, visualize the entity in question coming forth from your center and faring forth to a place at the outer extreme of the space you are making sacrosanct.

CLOSING RITE

After all of your operative work is concluded, in order to give a sense of definitely closing off the working time and space, you should have a set phrase and gesture. This need not be elaborate. Again many such formulas are found in more basic books.[150] The more advanced one becomes the less elaborate the rites need to be.

Clasp your hands before you, lower your arms to a 45-degree angle, imitative of the ᛉ-rune,[151] and say:

So shall it be!

Svá skall þat vera!

[svo skall það vera]

This can then be followed with the pronunciation of the word *alu* [AH-loo].

CONCLUSION

Magical operations take place in defined space and time. The reason for this is that magic is about changing or transforming things or events. In order to transform something, one must separate it from its stubborn solidified state, remold it, and return it to a new solidified state which is different from its previous one. Frame rituals are key components in effecting this separation and return.

Methods

In the process of meta-communication, certain methods must be applied to execute and transmit the message. Once the method has been mastered—both inner and outer—then any operation can be undertaken in an effective manner. Here we discuss the methods of *how* traditional meta-communications are composed and transmitted.

Execution in the physical world: There are two main ways to perform an act of operative runic communication in the physical world—through sign and speech. That is, when the physical sign is made—be it by carving, writing, painting, or gesture—it is *usually* accompanied by an auditory performance. (This was traditionally done in the softest of whispers.)

Semiotically, if one wishes to have an effect in the physical universe, a physical sign is a fitting anchor for that phenomenon. The fact that an inscription is carved into granite is in and of itself a *sign* of the intention of the runemaster for the effect of that inscription to be *permanent* or *eternal*.

On the other hand, if one wishes to have a subtle spiritual effect or influence—perhaps of a temporary kind—perhaps a less permanent sign needs to be made.

RUNE-RISTING

To rist the runes is to impress their stave shapes and idea content into the universe. This can be done by carving or writing them, or by signing their shapes in the air, or even by strongly visualizing them in the mind's eye.

Runes are most typically carved (into wood, bone, metal, or stone), but they can also simply be written or painted (on the same media plus paper or parchment). Even if carved, most runes are most often also colored or painted as well.

In any and all events, when runes are executed physically, they must also be effected *mentally* or *spiritually*. This is accomplished first and foremost through concentration and visualization. One must *execute consciously*. What is meant by this is that one must pour into the form (*shape/sound*) of the rune the *meaning* of the rune as one has come to understand it through deep meditative work on the lore.

You should practice executing runes in various media—writing, carving, painting, and so on. Do this until you are comfortable in this process. Then practice infusing the shapes with consciousness—with meaning.

RUNE-SENDING

Creating the runic medium of communication is only half of the process; one must also know how to transmit, or send (ON *senda*), the message which has been encoded in a medium. Sending can be accomplished in a variety of ways. In general sending is achieved through how the physical medium is treated at the conclusion of the rite—is it put in a certain place, burned, buried, something else?

Steadfasting

Steadfasting is the art of placing a runic medium (a stone, a wooden pole, etc.) in the right location so that it may remain fixed there for the duration of the effect you wish the working to have. Most important here is the choice of location. Here is where art enters the process. Is the purpose of your working to have a public effect? Is it meant to change the world in a *direct* way? Then it needs to be publicly visible. Is it meant to affect a certain person only? Then it needs to be placed where that person lives—in his house, or on her person, etc. In ancient times, when runemasters wished to immortalize a person being memorialized by a runestone, they often put the stone in a location where many people would see it regularly—on roadsides, at bridges, and so on, not necessarily anywhere close to the person's grave mound at all.

Casting

A common method of influencing a person or place in a more subtle or temporary manner is casting or throwing a runic medium into a certain location. It could be thrown or put into a person's house, or onto their property, or in their general direction. In olden times curses could be tossed under a person's seat at the table.[152] (As a pop-culture side note to this idea, I refer to the M. James short story entitled "Casting the Runes," which was made into the 1957 film *Curse of the Demon*, in England, also called *Night of the Demon*.) Or, more nobly, a spear (perhaps carved with runes) could be cast over an enemy army.

Burying

The general concept of hiding a runic inscription as a mode of sending is fundamental. Why? Because the region and activities of the divine or causal realm are for the most part hidden from us, placing communications in the channel of the hidden by concealing them is a semiotically valid way of working. This act of hiding may come in the form of complex codes, which hide meaning, or be effected by carving runes in hidden places—high in rafters, on the backs of brooches, etc. Most directly, they may be buried under the earth. If certain types of metal (iron objects, for example) are buried or if wooden objects are likewise put under the earth, they also undergo a *slow* process of disintegration into the earth. Metal rusts, and wood rots. During this process the runic message is slowly being sent through chthonic channels to do its work. On the other hand, when a stone is buried underground, it is meant to be simply hidden in the subterranean world to send a constant or eternal message in that realm.

Submerging

A close corollary to burying a runic object in the earth as a way of sending its message is that of submerging it in water or mud. Obviously, here it is a matter of communicating with the realm of water and its inhabitants. In ancient Germanic times ponds, small lakes, wells, springs, and bogs were favorite cultic sites where the human and numinous realms interacted. The nature or character of the sacred site should always resonate with the character of the operative message. One would not place a curse formula in a site sacred to a goddess of healing, for example. Always take the path of least resistance when practicing magic—the operation is likely to be more successful if you do.

Burning

One of the most effective and quick ways of sending a runic message is by burning the medium. In this way the message is sent at once. Obviously, in order to effect this mode of sending, one must execute the runic message on a flammable medium—paper, parchment, or wood. A pragmatic manner of doing one of these sendings is to carve the operative message into the wax of a candle and then burn the candle. As the message is burned upward and away, the communication is sent. Most operative runic objects made of wood were eventually burned as a way of sealing their sending, and so the objects could not later be profaned.

Swallowing

If one wishes to send a runic message into the interior of one's own, or someone else's, psychosomatic complex, then a useful technique involves actually ingesting or swallowing the medium. This can be effected in a wide variety of ways. The message can be carved into a small digestible object and swallowed like a pill. Or it can be carved on a larger object, such as a slice of cheese, etc., and consumed.[153] Inscriptions can also be made on more solid objects; then the inscription is scraped off in fine fragments or shavings and these are mixed with a symbolic drink and the whole swallowed for the same effect.[154] Similarly, runic messages can be written on parchment or paper, and then washed off into water with the water subsequently drunk. These latter techniques point to the fact that the inscription can be scraped off as a way to negate the power of the inscription, but that the now jumbled inscription can be reconstituted in another realm—in the interior realm of the body.

Hanging

One of the most conspicuous aspects of Germanic sacrificial ritual was the frequent practice of hanging victims or other symbolic objects in trees or from poles. The sacrifice itself is a form of communication entirely analogous in theory and form to many runic customs. Obviously, just as the physical elements of fire, water, or earth might be used as channels for meta-communication, with the practice of hanging objects the element of *air* is being used to convey the message. Objects are hung by leather strips, string, or twine and allowed to move about in the wind. Eventually, they will fall to the ground and be absorbed by the earth.

As you can see, the art and practice of sending can be complex. It consists of utilizing a mode of sending which resonates with the willed purpose of the runic communication.

CHAPTER FIVE

RUNE-WORKINGS: OPERATIONS OF RUNIC META-COMMUNICATION

 We will now explore a wide variety of methods of operation with practical examples for each method. Sometimes more than one concrete example must be given in order to illustrate the principles of the method fully. I should emphasize again that at more advanced stages of operative runology, the magician or runer is free to undertake various methods in order to effect runic communication. Each of these methods must be mastered, so the operations here can be seen as examples of the runic art and science.

Rune Tokens

Rune tokens are small movable objects made of stone, bone, wood, or metal which bear runic formulas. The foreign terms for such things would include "talismans" or "amulets." However, remember that the use of such terms can lead us astray from the inherent meaning of runic tokens.

Our own Germanic terminology is rich in words for such objects. In Old Norse they can be known as a *hlútr*, "lot, talisman"; *taufr*, "magical charms"; or in Old English as a *lybesn*, "amulet"—referring to its ability to heal or harm by means of "medicine." Such objects could be made of natural substances or manufactured ones; they could be concealed on the person, often in pouches hung around the neck, or worn openly. The only methodological guideline is that the object is to be created in harmony with its purpose and that its mobility allows it to be put in the place where it is to do its work.

Let's look at four examples of tokens: one for good luck (*auja*), one for healing or good health, one to exert influence, and one to curse an enemy.

TO GAIN GOOD LUCK

Good luck, the power of good fortune, comes with general personal power. Conventionally, this is gained through the accumulation of good and virtuous acts. This is generally how *hamingja*, "luck, power," is built up in a person's life. However, in the art and science of operative runology, there are methods of enhancing this power in mysterious ways.

One way to create a token of good luck is to take a strip of hardwood, about two inches in length, and into it carve the runes:

$$ХІᛒᚢ ᚠᚢᚠᚠ$$

Then color them red. Carry this stave with you always. It can be worn in a small pouch on a cord around your neck so that the inscription is near your heart.

An alternative inscription in English and English runes is:

$$:ᛁ: ᚸᛁᚻᛖ: ᚷᚠᛗ: ᚦᚢᚼᚼ:$$

Remember that the key to a successful operation lies in the concentration given to the execution of each individual rune in the spirit of the meaning of that rune.

HEALING OR GOOD HEALTH

A traditional ancient formula for healing and good health is that of *līn-laukaR*: "flax-leek." You can carve this formula on a bone and wear it in a pouch around your neck so no one can see it:

ᛚᛁᚾᛚᚨᚢᚲᚨᛉ

Another more straightforward way would be to write the formula: "I am healthy" in English runes:

:ᛁ:ᚫᛗ:ᚻᛠᛚᚦᚣ:

This can be written or carved and always kept on your person.

TO INFLUENCE OTHERS

Some people may balk at the idea of magically influencing others. However, as we have explained in the course of this work, magic is a form of *communication*. Whether in speech or writing, each time you attempt to convince another person to accept your viewpoint, or do something in your favor, you are practicing what the ancient Greeks called *rhetoric*. This is the art of using language, or any form of communication, to persuade another person. At its root, that is the nature of this magic. Of course, individuals would have to create their own customized formulas for situations that might arise. However, the tradition knows several examples of general formulas meant to win or gain favorable treatment from those who have the power to help us.

Carve or write this formula and have it on your person at all times:

:ᚻᛠᚱᚣᛖᚫᚾᛞᚻᛖᛞᛗᚣᚹᛁᛋᚻᛖᛋ:

This formula, which reads "Hear ye and heed my wishes," becomes a lever to open the event horizon to the flow of your heartfelt wishes for favorable influence over others.

A CURSE FORMULA

Even more controversial might be idea of practicing a curse. In essence, this is a hostile communication. Human beings engage in these on a daily basis. They are almost always counterproductive, because they are usually hurled without conscious thought and without awareness of the idea of justice. It is because we feel our curses are impotent that we cast them so readily. Once one decides to send a curse in a formal and considered way as an act of hostile magical communication, one almost always withdraws the idea as unwise. There are those times and situations, however, in which such an operation is justified.

Carve or write this formula on a medium—wood, bone, or parchment:

ᚠᛡᛁᛋᛏᛈᛗᛁᚾᚢᚱᛚᛈᚱᛗᚢᚱᛋᛗᛋ᛬ᚦᚦᚦ

Put the object in a place where the person to be cursed often walks or goes. To ensure that the curse will only be effective if it is held to be justified by the gods, carve or write the rune ᛏ on the object as well.

The Magical Comb

An operation peculiar to the runic tradition is the use of magical combs. The purpose of them is to strengthen the good fortune, or luck (*hamingja*), of an individual. The metaphysics of this lies in beliefs concerning the hair. For the ancient Germanic peoples, the hair was thought to be the repository of one's luck or the personal power—technically known in Old Norse as *hamingja*—of the individual. Taking care of one's luck involved taking care of one's hair. Being sure the inner world was in order often meant washing and combing the hair. Women often did this for their Viking chieftain husbands. This belief may explain why we find so many combs inscribed with runes. The runes used can either be intended to strengthen the *hamingja* or identify the individual for whom the comb is to work. So either the ᚷᛁᛒᚢ ᚠᚢᚦᚨ formula can be inscribed on the comb, or the name of the individual using the comb, making use of the standard mode of transliterating modern English into runes. One can even identify the comb as belonging to a person, for example, to say "(This is) Mark's comb," you inscribe:

ᛗᚲᚱᛉᛋᛉᚠᛗᛒ

When the hair is combed, concentrate on the right ordering of one's luck and power. The principle here is that no matter what quantity of this substance one possesses, having it in optimal order is a great advantage. From these ancient beliefs one can trace the modern obsession with hair. They are also behind why witch-finders usually shaved the heads of suspected witches before questioning them—for fear of the power residing there.

Spear-Casting

An archaic ritual for cursing an opponent in a religious way consisted of casting or throwing a spear over them or in their direction just before battle. This act is memorialized in the Eddic lines:

Fleygði Óðinn   *ok í fólk um skaut:*
þat var enn fólkvíg   *fyrst í heimi . . .*

Óðinn let fly   a shot over the army:
that was then a battle   the first in the world . . .

Actual artifacts, e.g., the spear of Kragehul, seem to be remnants of such a ritual.

The point of the rite was to dedicate—give—or in other words *sacrifice* the enemy to the gods. This meant that they belonged "to the gods," i.e., the otherworld, and no longer to *this world*. They were henceforth dispatched to the beyond, symbolically speaking.

In the ritual proposed here, we use a symbolic representation, not of a human enemy, but of an idea or whole group of people, nation, etc. Prepare a symbol suitable to this purpose and set it up in a wide-open space outdoors. Also prepare a throwing spear—it need not be fitted with an iron spearhead; a sharpened shaft of four to five feet in length and the approximate diameter of a broom handle will do. On the shaft carve a runic formula which indicates that you are dedicating the entity symbolized in front of you to the gods. An example might be:

ᛏᚠᚦᛖ᛫ᚠᛗᚺᛁ᛫ᚷ ᚢᚠᚾ꞉ ᚷ

This formula reads: "To the gods I g(ive) you," and to it is appended a bind-rune: ᚷ —here to be interpreted as the formula "(I) give you to the ᚠ = ōs = Wōden."

In a meditative state, throw the shaft in such a way that it arcs directly over the symbol and sticks into the ground beyond.

Carving and Scraping

We are obviously well informed about the carving of runes into objects. There are also a few references to the technique of scraping the runes off of an object in order to "deactivate" them. However, the scrapings still contain the power of the inscribed runes in potential. These scrapings of fine wood or powdered bone or soft stone can then be ingested by the magician in order to internalize the power of the runes, making them part of the rune-operator's own being. Such workings concentrate on permanent changes one wishes to make to one's own being. Examples would be things such as:

꞉ ᛁ ꞉ ᚠᛗ ꞉ ᛋᚱᚠᚷ꞉

I am strong

: | :ᛖᛗ : ᚹᛁᛋᛗ:
I am wise

These are affirmative formulas one would want to etch into one's being. What should be avoided in this kind of operation are temporary goals, or things which may only be fleeting in one's life.

This type of operation is an exercise in the specific method of sending whereby the runestaves are ingested in a disorganized state, to be reconstructed into a meaningful sending within the psychophysical complex of the magician. In the book *Nine Doors of Midgard* (Rûna-Raven, 2002), I illustrated the internal streams within the human body keyed to Germanic cosmology. Once a runic formula has been introduced into the psychophysical system of the individual, it will be sent to the corresponding internal features to effect the sending.

All sorts of runic affirmations, such as the ones above, and formulas of power and enlightenment can be internalized in this way. This is the mystery of the Catholic eucharist, culled from ancient Roman ritual practice—inherited from Indo-European tradition. But here, in the practice of *magic*, the will and intent of the individual magician is determinative, not a preexisting religious aim.

Especially effective forms of this sort of magic involve the assimilation of divine attributes. An example of this would be the absorption of the attributes of inspiration embodied in the name of the god Wōðanaz. This can be done by carving the formula **wodanaz** in runes, scraping them off into a suitably symbolic drink, and ingesting the runes in their blended state. The runes for the name of the god appear:

ᚹᛟᛞᚨᚾᚨᛉ

At the moment the runic formula is swallowed, the runes should be strongly visualized and the name repeated three times.

Bind-Runes

In the beginning bind-runes, the combination of two or more runic shapes into one figure, might have been used by rune-masters to save space in their inscriptions. They were a kind of abbreviation. But these bind-runes soon took on a meaning of their own. They are combinations of two or more sets of runic connotations into a single expression. Their shapes are preferably pleasing to the eye, as symmetrical as possible, not too ornate, and sometimes illegible to outsiders trying to tell the intention of the working. Ideally, the overt intention of the shape will also be lost to the conscious mind of the creator as the bind-rune takes on a synthesized meaning of its own, unique and powerful, intelligible only to the gods.

Any symbolically meaningful word can be rendered as a bind-rune formula. Any of the languages can be used—ancient or modern. Here follow four examples of bind-rune work.

The first two examples of bind-runes are drawn from the actual runic record. Bind-runes could be made when adjacent runes could share a single mainstave: ⌶. For example ᛗ and ᛙ could be combined to ᛙ = *em*, "I am." or one shape could be combined with another in other creative ways.

The spear of Kragehul gives us the bind-rune ✕, which has been seen as representative of the formulaic *gibu auja*, "I give good luck." A very similar example also occurs on the Anglo-Frisian bracteate of Undley: ✕ = *go* or *og*.

gibu auja

Place this symbol anywhere to focus the power of good luck in that place, or wear it on your person.

Another more spiritual example is that of the combination of **a** and **R** or **z**. -aR is a frequent combination in older runic inscriptions, because it is a common grammatical ending. The symbolic values of these runes are oriented toward idealized spiritual power, so the combination of them into the form below is potent:

Note that in the creation of bind-runes upward or downward orientations seem less important than an aesthetic combination. This is a sign of reorienting one's life and focus of life toward the gods, toward the sovereign god of inspiration and consciousness.

For cultivating the mental trait of wakefulness, to remind yourself to be awake and aware at all times—from a deep and unconscious level—the word *awake* can be rendered first into runes: ᚲᚹᚨᚾᛗ , then combined into a bind-rune:

Other designs are, of course, also possible. That is the beauty and mystery of the practice.

To instill a strong will, one can bring to bear one of the original three gods, Wiljōn, whose name means "strong will." A bind-rune made from his name can act as a catalyst to awaken this faculty in the individual magician. In older runes his name appears: ᚹᛁᛚᛃᛟᚾ , which can be combined into a bind-rune:

Again, such bind-runes can be stored in a secret place, sent in one of the various manners described earlier, or worn on the person in one way or another.

Rune-Gazing

This technique of performing a runic operation at first appears to be revolutionary. But in fact it was one of the simplest among ancient runemasters. It is basically the use of the power of strong visualization to etch the runes directly into the unconscious mind, and thus directly into the fabric and event horizon of the universe. This is done by visualizing each rune being "carved" in a red light into a white or black space.

We know that the Viking Age skalds composed poetry while lying in the dark—and that some of them, such as Egill Skallagrímsson, were also runemasters. It is not beyond the realm of possibility that runic composition was added to the magical and mnemonic devices employed by these masters of memory and magic. In the darkness the runes and the sounds they represented were permanently etched into the minds of these ancients. We know also that their compositions were handed down orally for generations—word for word—before finally being written down in the Middle Ages.[155]

It would probably be too much to expect that lengthy texts could be etched into the world by modern minds. However, even in our own stunted modernistic state, we can use shorter texts or single words in this way.

Runestone Carving

The most famous and conspicuous of all runic monuments are the magnificent runestones of Scandinavia. The rarest of these stem from the older runic period, while the vast majority are from the Viking Age and later. Most of them are memorial stones which honor a dead person. Also memorialized on the stone may be the sponsor of the stone, that is, the person most likely to have paid the runemaster to carve and erect it. Beyond this, the runemaster himself is frequently mentioned in a sort of master-signature formula: "X carved the runes." It is with these stones that the art of rune-carving reached its zenith in antiquity. Current runemasters may now also exercise a high level of artistic and magical power once they are freed to compose inscriptions in their own language.

Carving into stone brings great responsibility. Once something is "set in stone," it becomes permanent—or tends to be so. This is the power and the peril of runestone carving from the magical viewpoint. What is set in stone must be something which is perennially valuable and worthy of immortality. The chief subject of runestone magic is just this—the immortalization of people, events, and places. After studying this book, the reader will already have realized how this process is *magical*. Through rune-carving people are immortalized, events are made to have lasting effects, and places are sanctified.

There are few rules for effective runestone carving, but the ones that exist are important magically. Formulas should be brief, employ basic words with Germanic roots, follow traditional patterns of syntax, and be alliterative, if possible. The original reason why runic formulas were composed the way they were is because the ancestors believed these were the patterns found when the gods spoke to humans—briefly, simply, and poetically. We should "speak their language" when conversing not only with them, but also with the fabric of the universe. Here are three examples of formulas for three major types of runestone usages.

A MEMORIAL STONE

Memorial stones are not gravestones. They can be erected in grave fields (yards) or areas where the grave mounds exist, but they were more commonly displayed in other public areas—roadsides, open fields, at bridges, etc. The idea was to have strangers who knew how to read runes pass by and read the stone. Therefore, such formulas today could be placed anywhere. You may wish to memorialize your father who has passed away. He may be buried in another state, or his ashes may be in your home. The stone could be placed in a more conspicuous area, near someplace important to him, or it could be erected in your backyard garden.

Here is an example:

ᛗᚨᚱᚢᚾᚨᛑᚦᛁᛋ:ᛑ:ᚱᚨᛁᛋᛗᛑᚨᚠᛏᛗᚱ:ᚠᚱᚨᚾᚴ:ᚢᛗᚱᚠᚨᚦᛗᚱ
ᚢᛗᚠᚨᛋᚱᛟᚠᚠᛑ:ᛗ:

Mary had this st(one) raised after Frank her father. :
He was a good m(an).

To be noted are that there are two ideographic runes ᛑ and ᛗ both set off by double points, as the name of the man being memorialized. These are not rules, just flourishes of the runemaster's art.

MEMORIALIZING AN EVENT

Events to be memorialized are heroic events. Here is a contemporary and local example. In September of 2011 wildfires raged in Bastrop County, Texas. Ninety-five percent of the state park there was destroyed. The Rune-Gild had scheduled its Ninth World-Moot for this location in November of that year. The fires were bravely fought and eventually bested by firefighters. At the Moot members of the Gild memorialized this event by composing and executing a runestone which reads:

ᚢᛗᚱᛗᚦᛗᛒᚨᛚᛑᚠᚨᚢᚷᚢᛏᚦᛗᚠᛁᚱᛗᚯ

here the bold fought the fire + the ideogram ᛏ × 2

This stone can now be seen displayed in the park.

HALLOWING A STEAD

Runestones always hallow or sanctify the area in which they stand. Some actually seem to have this as their primary motive. In the Danish tradition we see that the god Thor was often invoked to hallow the runes, and the stone, and by extension to protect the area. This is because Thor is seen as the protector of the divine realm, and it is to this divine realm that the runes belong. An example of a simple inscription to create a permanently hallowed space would be:

ᚦᚢᛏᚲᚱᚾᚨᛚᚠᚹᚦᛁᛂᛁ ᛏᛈ

þunarhalowþisstead

Thunar hallow this stead!

By using a formula of this type, you can create a permanently hallowed and sanctified space for ritual work, and thus one that does not have to be re-sanctified each time it is used.

Besides inscriptions in stone, similar or identical formulas can be carved into wooden poles. Round poles with diameters or dimensions of between six and twelve inches were commonly erected at Germanic sacred sites, and such poles were also used as memorials. Of course, these would have decayed in a relatively few years, whereas the stones survive even unto this day. However, a wooden pole of oak or another hardwood could certainly last a lifetime. We have evidence for the erection of such poles in a few written sources. A good and informative example of this is found in *Ibn Fadlan's Travel Report*. There we read concerning the final preparations of a Viking funeral and ship burial:

> Next they build up a somewhat rounded hill-like mound over the position of the ship—which they had pulled up on shore out of the river—in the middle of the mound they erected a large beam of birchwood and wrote the

name of the man and the name of the king of the Rûs on it, then they went away.[156]

Clearly if they were writing, they were writing in runes. It would appear that in remote locations the Scandinavians would resort to other media for the execution of runic inscriptions. This reminds us of the wooden grave markers used instead of headstones in the American Old West.

The Magic of Writing and Reading Runes

Among the questions the Hávamál asks the would-be runemaster are: "Do you know how to write? Do you know how to read?" As we have already seen, the act of writing is clearly acknowledged as an active process. The magician can cause things to happen if his art and science are skillful enough to affect the event horizon. He writes words in runes and is responded to in phenomena. The concept of reading runes seems equally clear, but actually is more complex than most think. Reading runes could refer to the simple ability to decipher a runic text, or it could refer to the knowledge of how to use runestaves for divinatory purposes.[157]

Beyond these two considerations, there is a third dimension, deeply rooted in the ancient traditions of rune-carvers and the cultures which nurtured them. Reading a runic text seems to be a *passive* activity. In fact, reading can be an active endeavor in that it constitutes an act of cooperative magic between the writer and the reader. The writer plants a formulaic seed and it has its immediate effect perhaps, but if the text is visible to future would-be readers, moments will occur when the text will be read with knowing hearts and minds. When this reading is done, the effects and power of the text are once more vivified and renewed. The reader waters the seed of power.

These ideas are not the speculations of a modern magician. These concepts are clearly illustrated in many ancient runic inscriptions, both pagan and Christian. The formula that reveals the reality of this concept is exemplified by the medieval Vind-laus inscription from Norway, which reads in Old Norwegian:

þessar rúnar reist Vésteinn. Heill sá en reist,
ok svá bæði sá en ræðr

Vesteinn carved these runes. Good luck to him who carved
(them) as well as to him who reads (the runes).

This is typical of many others from the Viking Age, and here survives into the Christian era in its pagan form—imparting "good luck" (ON *heill*) for both the writer and the eventual reader(s) of the formula. Christianized versions of the formula will substitute the idea of "God bless him who carved the runes and him who reads them."

The full impact of the power of this formula and its implications are only completely manifest once one realizes that it is a way to tie generations of people together, bound in a specific esoteric tradition. The carver trusts that others will come along and read the text, and by doing so will continue and renew the good luck the original carver had worked out, and additionally, the reader will gain a similar magical boon through the act of *reading* the text. Time, space, and culture can be bridged by the utilization of this type of formula.

It must also be said that this idea—brought into its most stark and direct expression by this magical runic formula—is really an idea which is true for all writers and readers of all kinds of texts throughout history.

APPENDICES

RUNIC DYADS

The one who first devised the fuþark, and those who first made use of it, were most likely men who thought in a poetic fashion. Poetry and storytelling were most probably a good portion of their stock and trade as cultural artisans of verbal creations. Poetic thought, thought which forges connections between and among symbolic elements based on meaningful and aesthetic principles, could therefore plausibly be seen in how the originator of the runic system first arranged elements. Obviously, the elements of sound represented by signs (staves) were not ordered according to any linguistic criteria (such as we find in the arrangement of sounds and letters in the Sanskrit system). Here I seek to elucidate some possibilities with regard to the arrangement of the runestaves in meaningful pairs, or dyads.

Elsewhere[158] I have explored the theories of Elmar Seebold, a scholar who saw the origin of the order of the fuþark in a late antique mysto-magical technique referred to as Ath-bash. My own thoughts here are not so complex, nor are they as convoluted as those referred to by Seebold. Actually, what I propose is a relatively simple, if poetic, understanding of the relationships between pairs of runestaves immediately juxtaposed to one another in the rune-row.

These ideas were initially sparked in a conversation I had in the mid-1980s with Edgar Polomé, who first pointed out to me the connecting link between the first and second and the third and fourth rune-names.

The ideas briefly developed in this article will be further elaborated upon in my forthcoming book *The Rune-Names.*

At first glance there appears to be a certain connection between the concepts underlying the names of the runes as they are paired in the following fashion:

ᚠᚢ ᚦᚨ ᚱᚲ ᚷᚹ ᚺᚾ ᛁᛃ ᛇᛈ ᛉᛊ
ᛏᛒ ᛖᛗ ᛚᛜ ᛞᛟ

One of the most intriguing possibilities surrounding the study of runic dyads is that of elucidating unknown or questionable aspects of runic symbolism. Certain rune-names, specifically those for the **k-**, **w-**, **p-**, and **b-**runes, could at least in part be clarified by this dyadic theory of runic symbolism.

It will generally be found that each runic dyad will have some concept which binds the pair together and some decisive aspect which sharply distinguishes them from each other. This dichotomy between sameness (homogeneity) and difference (heterogeneity) in and of itself speaks of a certain poetic power.

The first two rune-names are *fehu*: "livestock, sheep" and *ūruz*: "aurochs." Both probably originally referred to zoological quadrupeds. They have the idea of symbolically important animal power which binds them together; they are different in that one is domestic (*fehu*) and the other wild (*ūruz*).

Þurisaz and *ansuz* are similarly connected in that they both represent greater-than-human powers. They might be called "numinous," although in the case of *þurisaz* this might be incorrect. In any event, they are sharply distinguished in that *þurisaz* represents a natural force, and is more often than not characterized as evil, while *ansuz* stands for a spiritual power, which is thought of as good.

These first two dyads appear so obvious—along with a few others (*hagalaz : nauðiz, īsa : jēra*, and *ehwaz : mannaz*)—that a certain groundwork is laid for further investigation.

The next two rune-names are *raiðō*: "riding, (wagon?)" and *kēnaz*: "torch." Questions abound with this pair. Does *raiðō* originally refer to a vehicle, the act of riding a horse, or both? Is the original name of the k-rune something which means "torch" (cf. OE *cēn*) or a "sore" (cf. ON *kaun*)? It should also be noted at this juncture that some scholars, such as Wolfgang Krause, have postulated that the runes had more than one name, which would be of benefit in divinatory practice. (See appendix B.) However, if the principles we are positing here are correct, it would appear possible that the dyad refers to the manifestation of certain skills: one having to do with either the mechanical construction of wagons, carts, chariots, or the training of horses, the other with pyrotechnical skills (metallurgy, etc.). This would lend credence to the idea that the original name of the k-rune was **kēnaz*, not **kaunaz*. The importance of the horse and equine technology in the symbolism of the rune-row speaks to the extremely archaic and culturally conservative nature of that symbolism harkening back to Indo-European times.

*Gēbō: "gift" and **wunjō*: "joy" form a dyad based on the principles of certain "social concepts." **Gēbō* is an exchange ("gift for gain"); it implies hospitality and even religious sacrifice (referred to most often in Norse sources as "giving"). This process of outer action—of giving and receiving in return—whether practiced between humans (e.g., gift-giving, hospitality) or between humans and gods (religious sacrifice) is itself reciprocated as an inner feeling = "joy." The very reciprocity of concepts may also be reflected in the phrases OE *mann byþ on myrgðe / his māgan lēof*: "man in his rejoicing is dear to his kinsman" and ON *maðr er manns gaman*: "man is the amusement or enjoyment of man(kind)." (Also see Hávamál 47.) In

both instances, it appears, productive and enjoyable human interaction is cited as a source of joy.

*Hagalaz: "hail" and *nauðiz: "need" form a dyad based on the concept of catastrophe or disaster. Hail obviously manifests itself in human life from above (from sky to earth) or from the outside inward, while *nauðiz is specifically referred to as an inner event (ON þungr or hneppr kostr or OE nearu on breostan) which naturally results in outer difficulties.

*Īsa and *jēra clearly can both be classified under the principle of natural conditions or phenomena of nature—ice (freezing) and the yearly ripening of plants suitable for harvest. What distinguishes them is obviously that the former is destructive or detrimental to growth, while the latter is productive and beneficial.

The precedent set elsewhere in the rune-row which seems to indicate that there is a principle of meaningful rune-pairings, or dyads, could help clarify the difficulty surrounding the meaning of the name of the fourteenth rune: perðrō. Fortunately, the rune-name with which it is paired, *eihwaz, can with certainty be identified as the yew tree. The yew is a tree with a rich symbolic lore.[159] It can safely be called a "sacred tree" in Germanic mythology. This makes it more likely that *perðrō originally referred to a tree which also bore sacred connotations but which contrasted with the yew in some essential point. The *perðrō ("pear"?) was probably a fruit-bearing (see Tacitus, Germania chapter 10), deciduous tree. Very late Icelandic evidence found in the málrúnakenningar[160] provide kennings for the letter /p/ which include several references to healing (e.g., græðing meina, "healing of injuries," and symsla-lækning, "ointment-medicine") and also to "fate" or the Norns (e.g., norna-sviði, "burning pain inflicted by the Norns"). This admittedly recent evidence, recorded in modern times, supports the idea that perðrō originally had something to do with the Norns, divination, fate, and healing. If Karl Schneider's bold interpretation "dice-box" is correct, it makes it likely that the box was fashioned out of *perðrō*-wood, as were the runestaves.

An analysis of the two rune-names **elhaz*: "elk" and **sowilō*: "sun" shows that both represent the highest, or most noble, and exalted of their respective classes—the terrestrial animal world for the elk and the sky for the sun. The association between "the highest" and the sun requires no further explanation, but the connection of the elk and this idea may need some clarification. An elk is considered the beast par excellence. In Indo-European times deer may have been domesticated before the horse. (Scythians "disguised" their horses as deer for ceremonial purposes.) Later mythic material relating to Sigurðr/Siegfried (the greatest or highest of all heroes) link him repeatedly with the deer or hind. In the *Þiðreks saga* (chapter 162), he is fostered by hinds; when he kills Fáfnir, he tries to disguise his name at first by calling himself the *göfugt dýr* ("noble beast"), which is a well-attested kenning for a stag (Fáfnismál 2), and finally when he awakens the *valkyrja*, he does so after ascending a mountain called Hindarfjell (hind-mountain). As an aside, it might be noted that in these three references to the deer or elk there could be a reflection of the three functions identified by Dumézil: birth (fertility)—dragon-slaying—awakening of the higher self and initiation into runes.

The dyadic pairing of **teiwaz* and **berkanō* lends some clarity to the symbolic meaning of **berkanō*. **Teiwaz* is obviously the divine name for the god ON Týr, OE Tīw, or for a god in general (*týr* is used in this way in Old Norse, for example). The exact meaning of **berkanō* has been problematic due to the suffix -*an*-. It is not the word for the birch tree. This would be simply **berkō*. In ON the word for birch is *björk*, whereas the name for the runestave is *bjarkan*. Karl Schneider, to some extent following Carl Marstrander, identified **berkanō* as "the birch goddess."

Linguistically, this might be explained as a feminine form of the -*an*- suffix, which in words such as PGmc. **Wōð-an-az or Go. *þiud-in-as* ("king") indicates the "master of" or "master over" something. Thus the dyad would come under the heading of divinity, distinguished by the transcendent sky orientation of the **teiwaz* and the immanent earth orientation of **berkanō.*

One of the most obvious and strongest dyads in the rune-row is that of *ehwaz* : *mannaz* (horse : man). These are two contrasting forms of active beings, the horse being a manifestation of physical power, *mannaz*: "human being" as a manifestation in Midgard of intellectual power and consciousness, man and horse form a unit. The horse provides power, speed, and mobility; the man provides thought, guidance, and purpose (informed by the gods, of course).

The dyad formed by the l- and **ng**-runes has a meaning that depends on the original name of the l-rune. Most consider that this was *laguz*: "water." Wolfgang Krause thought that it could have been *laukaz*: "leek." In fact, perhaps, the runes had a system of various names. If the dyad is *laguz* : *ingwaz*, then the unifying principle is infinity—the infinite sea and the infinite earth. Whereas if the dyad is *laukaz* : *ingwaz*, the unifying principle is growth—distinguished between organic growth and divine growth.

Finally, the dyad of *dagaz* : *oðila* has to do with limits or borders—the first of heaven or the sky and of time, the other of earth and space.

In conclusion, I would like to emphasize that these ideas could be expanded upon greatly. Each rune in such a dyad helps illuminate its dyadic partner. It is my considered opinion that this model does not entirely represent a contemporary esoteric speculation, but rather reflects actual ancient lore concerning the runes as they were contemplated by the earliest runemasters who must have viewed the runic system with the eyes of poets.

TRIADIC RUNE-NAMES

ᚠ	*fehu* (cattle)	*faihiþō* (feud)	*fūri* (fire)
ᚢ	*ūruz* (aurochs)	*ūrjan* (semen)	*ūra* (drizzle)
ᚦ	*þurisaz* (giant)	*þurnuz* (thorn)	*þiuða* (the good)
ᚨ	*ansuz* (ancestral god)	*aikaz* (oak)	*alu* (ale)
ᚱ	*raiðō* (wagon)	*rēðaz* (advice)	*rehitaz* (law)
ᚲ	*kēnaz* (torch)	*kwerðraz* (fire-bore)	*kaunaz* (sore)
ᚷ	*gēbō* (gift)	*galgōn* (gallows)	*gaizaz* (spear)
ᚹ	*wunjō* (joy)	*wunja* (pasture)	*wulhwaz* (wolf)
ᚺ	*hagalaz* (hail)	*hagiz* (hedge)	*hurnaz* (horn)
ᚾ	*nauðiz* (need)	*nabō* (hub [of wheel])	*naglaz* (nail)
ᛁ	*īsa* (ice)	*īsarno* (iron)	*ītraz* (the excellent one)
ᛃ	*jēra* (year)	*jestuz* (yeast)	*jēnaz* (stroke [of a scythe])
ᛇ	*ïhwaz* (yew)	*ïwaz* ([yew] bow)	*iðiz* (deed)
ᛈ	*perðrō* (pear tree)	*paðaz* (path)	*plōguz* (plough)
ᛉ	*elhaz* (elk)	*alhaz* (temple)	*algiz* (swan)
ᛋ	*sowilō* (sun)	*stainaz* (stone)	*slangō* (snake)
ᛏ	*tīwaz* (god)	*triuwiðō* (loyalty)	*taiknaz* (sign)
ᛒ	*berkanō* (birch goddess)	*berhtō* (f. bright one)	*brugjō* (bridge)
ᛖ	*ehwaz* (horse)	*eburaz* (boar)	*eðaraz* (fence)
ᛗ	*mannaz* (man)	*mēnon* (the moon)	*medu* (mead)
ᛚ	*laguz* (water)	*laukaz* (leek)	*laþu* (invitation)
ᛜ	*ingwaz* (earth god)	*angaz* (grief)	*wangaz* (meadow)
ᛞ	*dagaz* (day)	*daigaz* (dough)	*duskaz* (twilight)
ᛟ	*ōþila* (property)	*ōsaz* (river mouth)	*ōberaz* (edge)

GRAIL MYTHOS IN OLD ENGLISH RUNES?

As we have seen, the Anglo-Saxons expanded the runic futhark to an eventual total of thirty-three runestaves. They were using as many as twenty-nine from the earliest period for which we have records for them (ca. 450 CE). In essence this system is simply an expansion of the twenty-four-character Fuþark.

Also from an early time (ca. 700–800 CE) two runes not belonging to these twenty-nine, ᛣ *calc*: "chalice" used to represent the "hard" /c/ as in "cup" and ᚸ *gâr*: "spear" for the "hard" /g/ as in "gar," were occasionally being used. For one to two hundred years earlier the related Frisian tradition on the Continent was using an additional rune: ᛥ *stân* for /st/. However, in one manuscript—the Cotton MS Domitian A9 of the eleventh century—which is probably the clearest, most reliable representation of the codified English tradition preserved in the eleventh and twelfth centuries (ca. 1000–1200 CE), we find these runes not only present but juxtaposed to one another along with their names:

ᛣ	ᛥ	ᚸ
calc	*stân*	*gâr*
cup	stone	spear

I find it more than coincidental that these three elements would be juxtaposed with one another in an ostensibly "secret tradition" at a time and in a place reputed to have been a hot-bed of Grail mysticism. That precisely these three elements—a chalice, a stone, and a spear (of Longinus)—are essential to the thirteenth-century German poet Wolfram von Eschenbach's esoteric vision of the Grail he presents in his epic poem *Parzivâl* is remarkable. Wolfram also sees the Grail more as a stone (one said to have "heathen writing" appear on it as instructions to the Grail knights). All of this seems too much to ignore.

As we noted in the section on *calc* in the body of this book, it may well be an *interpretatio Christiana* for the older symbol of the horn—as the sacred drinking vessel in Germanic religious ritual. The stone would be the stone into which such runes are carved to give them their eternal, timeless form and send their messages over time—while the spear is that of Woden.

Some may be confused to some extent by what seems to be the Christian symbolism of the Grail—however, the astounding fact is that there was originally absolutely nothing Christian about it. Only some of the less enlightened myths of its origins (not that of Wolfram/Kyôt, for example) are Christianized—but these seem late and apologetic. The actual way in which the Grail and its order function is precisely un- or counter-Christian, i.e., Christ is not a factor and the established church is not involved with it. An earthly high priest or initiate is cho-sen from the Order of Knights to act as Grail king in service of the purely abstract (nonpersonal) principles represented by the Grail. It is no wonder the whole Grail mythos was shunned by the medieval Church—there was simply no Christ in it.

It seems that the "magical formula" *calc-stân-gâr* actually represents an esoteric understanding of the Grail mythos which was well-developed in the Germanic world. Although Wolfram refers to southern sources from Moorish Spain, no hard evidence for this understanding has actually come from there. So we are left with Wolfram's lengthy discourses in *Parzivâl* as well as other discussions in medieval German works, e.g., the *Wartburgkrieg* of Heinrich von Ofterdingen, in which the Grail is also identified with a stone that fell from Lucifer's crown, and the Old English runic tradition, as sources for the chalice-stone-spear complex. Thus it may well be that this whole constellation of symbols actually represents a heathen tradition in a heterodox Christian setting. It is not far-fetched to assume that heathen elements would find a safer home in heretical ideas than in trying to wedge themselves into orthodox forms (although this also happened).

It may also be possible that the ultimate origin of this symbolic complex is among the Alans, a North Iranian tribe. The Romans are known to have settled a military contingent of these warriors in the northern part of what became England and southern Scotland during the time that regions of Britain were part of the Roman Empire. When the Romans moved out around 400 CE, they left these warriors behind and they continued as a separate, but influential community for some time. Notably the three runes in question occur first in the Northumbrian region, a region under the influence of these Alans. It is to this tribal name that the English surname "Allen" or "Alan" is ascribed. The Alans are closely related to the Scythians, about whom Herodotus reports in the fifth century that at the origin of their tribe certain golden objects fell from the sky: a plow and yoke, a battle-ax and a cup. These obviously related to the three Dumézilian functions: fertility, war, and priestcraft. Could the complex cup-stone-spear have a similar meaning? Could these have been the Alanic version of a myth similar to that of their brother Scythians? If so, we have the three functions: stone = earth, spear = war, and cup = priestcraft.

Another possible link to these symbols is provided by Irish myth. In the text of the *Second Battle of Mag Tured*,[161] we learn of certain mythical realms and specific objects ascribed to them. These are four in number, and the relevant text reads:

> The Tuatha De Danann lived in the northern isles of the world, learning lore and magic and druidism and wizardry and cunning until they surpassed the sages of the arts of heathendom. There were four cities in which they learned lore and science and diabolic arts, to wit Falias, Gorias, Murias and Findas. Out of Falias was brought the stone of Fal, which was in Tara. It used to roar under every king that would take the realm of Ireland. Out of Gorias was brought the spear that Lug had. No battle was ever won against it or him who held it in his hand. Out of Findas was brought the sword of Nuada. When it was drawn from its deadly sheath, no one ever escaped from it, and it was irresistible. Out of Murias was brought the Dagda's Cauldron. No company ever went from it unthankful.

In any event, it appears that the three objects in question here: the cup, stone, and spear must be examined as a triadic complex of symbols. I think this material is sufficient for any operative runologist to be able to unravel the significance of the *calc-stân-gâr* complex—perhaps with the one additional piece of information that the spear is certainly Gungnir, the spear of Wotan which acts as his scepter of power—the true "spear of destiny." The reader is invited to explore ideas surrounding East Germanic spearheads found the book *The Mysteries of the Goths* (Rûna-Raven, 2007).

NOTES

1   My researches into the *Armanen* tradition in the 1970s included the study of most of the works of Guido von List as well as *Die Hochzeit der Menschheit* by Rudolf John Gorsleben. Most influential at the very earliest stage was, however, *Runenmagie* by Karl Spiesberger.

2   See *History of the Rune-Gild* III, pp. 33–46.

3   For a survey of Indo-European mythology see Jaan Puhvel, *Comparative Mythology* (Baltimore: Johns Hopkins, 1987) and on the idea of using these ideas in a contemporary way, see my article "How to Be a Heathen" printed in *Blue-Rûna* (Rûna-Raven, 2001, pp. 1–16).

4   For a virtually complete catalog of these practices, see my book *Runes and Magic* (Lang, 1986). A third, improved and expanded edition of this once rare volume has appeared with Rûna-Raven Press (2010).

5   The word "world" is derived from Old English *werold*, which literally means the "age of man." It refers to a psycho-cosmological concept which answers directly to the Greek term αιων—*aion* or "eon."

6   To study texts from an etymological perspective, one must have access to books such as Jan de Vries's *Altnordisches etymologisches Wörterbuch*. This allows you to look

at words historically, or diachronically (through time), rather than just as petrified definitions.

7   See Vilhelm Grönbech, *Culture of the Teutons* (London: Oxford University Press, 1931).

8   See Cleasby-Vigfusson, p. 504.

9   See Bosworth and Toller, p. 804.

10   For a discussion of the OHG terminology, see Wesche (1940: 45–51).

11   See Streitberg, vol II, p. 112.

12   The Finnish word "rune" refers to a "series" of things, e.g., one in the series of songs in the *Kalevala*; it is not the same word as *rūnō*, "mystery," although it too is one of the some 800 words borrowed into Finnish from Proto-Germanic.

13   The phrase "Welsh grain" requires some explanation. The word "welsh" was used by the Germanic peoples to denote foreigners whose speech they could not understand. At different times it might be used with regard to the Celts or the Romans. The Anglo-Saxons used it for the Cymru, hence our modern use of the term "Welsh." Originally, the Germanic people took tribute from foreigners in the form of grain; as gold began to be paid by more wealthy nations, "grain" became a poetic code word for gold. During the time when this bracteate was manufactured (sometime after 450) a good deal of gold was coming north from Rome—perhaps even as a part of

the treasure taken by Alaric the Visigoth after his sacking of Rome in 410.

14   One scholar developed an etymology which connects PGmc. *rūn-* *w*ith an IE word for "cut" or "carve." While this etymology connects the Germanic and Celtic word to a wider IE context, it does not explain the semantics of the word as it actually appears in Germanic and Celtic dialects. The plain fact that *rūnō* did not originally indicate merely a "written (or carved) character" is clearly reflected by the reality that the word *rún* (and its many derivatives) cannot be limited by this concrete, and if you will pardon the pun, literal, definition.

15   Anyone interested in this level of study should consult any good textbook on Germanic philology or historical linguistics.

16   All definitions are taken from the dictionary of Cleasby-Vigfusson.

17   There is a forthcoming monograph entitled *Rúnarmál III* from Rûna-Raven on the word "rune" and all the various forms the root *rūn-* takes in the Germanic languages.

18   This reference is found in *History of the Goths* (XXIV [121]).

19   The term "operative" refers to the fact that a subject or "doer" of an action is conceived of as being able to make changes or modifications in the environment based on the form the communicative act takes.

20   This concept is more fully developed in the pages of *Rúnarmál I*.

21   For a survey of these terms, see Flowers, *Runes and Magic*, pp. 85ff.

22   The text of *Runes and Magic* extensively develops the idea of magic as an act of communication in a scientific manner. The relevant sections in this book are based on that and other texts.

23   See Cleasby-Vigfusson, pp. 158; 165.

24   *Radical* or *synthetic runologists* are those who have no inner conflict between objective and subjective "definitions." As a radical runologist, or "rune-magician," one should not be baffled by the scholarly discussion of magic (from an anthropological perspective) nor should the scholarly definition of magic be one which does not take into account the cultural and philosophical validity and reality of the practice of magic in societies of all kinds.

25   See the Flowers article "Magic" in *Medieval Scandinavia: An Encyclopedia,* pp. 399–400.

26   For a review of the term *alu*, see Flowers, *Runes and Magic*, pp. 170–74.

27   See Polomé 1954 and 1996.

28   Bracteates are thin gold disks that originally were imitations of Roman coins. There was an influx of gold into

Scandinavia after the sack of Rome by the Germanic Visigoths in 410.

29   Although there may or may not have been a doctrine of gematria in the runic tradition in ancient times, in contemporary usage many magicians have applied this ideology to good effect.

30   The Uþark theory was first suggested by the Swedish philologist Sigurd Agrell. It does not seem to be a tenable theory as to the origin of the runes, but it could be that the "uþark" represented a later code for the practice of gematria, whereby the normal numerical value of the rune was shifted one place to the right. When this is done, there are remarkable correspondences with the numerical lore of the Greco-Roman world.

31   Works which better treat runic history are *Runelore* (Weiser, 1986) and *The Rune-Poems* (Rûna-Raven, 2002).

32   The methods for doing this, at least at the basic level, are outlined in the essay "How to Be a Heathen" published in *Blue Rûna* (Rûna-Raven, 2001).

33   *Rúnatals þattr Óðins* is the name given to the section of the Hávamal (stanzas 138–65) which outlines Óðinn's reception of the runes and his first uttering of runic teaching.

34   The technology and rationale for the Odinic sacrifice are archaic and purely traditional in origin. A reflection of the old methods of performing this sacrifice are alluded to in the *Gautreks saga* (chapter 7). The supposed similarities to the crucifixion of Jesus are merely coincidental and superficial.

35   This topic is discussed in *Runes and Magic*, pp. 18–20, and the bibliography given there is valuable to this topic.

36   This inscription may or may not be runic.

37   This idea did not have its origins in Nazi Germany, as some might suppose, but rather goes back to the Swedish Gothicists, such as Olof Rudbeck.

38   For a convenient overview of these, see Elliott (1989).

39   This sentiment was perhaps fueled by the general animosity some felt for things "Roman."

40   The Negau helmet is discussed in Elliott, *Runes*, pp. 9–11.

41   This consistency in ancient times is in marked contrast to the history of the runic revival in the late twentieth century when early on there was a general confusion about basic lore due to the variety of nontraditional approaches. At this juncture it seems that most of the faddists have gone elsewhere and the tradition has begun to reassert itself. The general confusion that reigned in the early phase of the current runic revival (post 1980) stemmed from the fact that dabblers and exploiters "made stuff up" with no reference to any actual tradition. A *true* runic revival recognizes the prestige of tradition and the need for hierarchy. The unwise left to their own devices create a cacophony of senseless babble.

42   For the most comprehensive approach to the runes on this level, see *Runes and Magic* (Rûna-Raven, 2010).

43 We see such speculations in ancient ties among Greek philosophers, such as Plato and Pythagoras, and after them the Hebrew Kabbalists take up a similar type of speculation and "literal mysticism."

44 Bracteates, disks of thin gold embossed with images of a religious or mythic character used in an amuletic fashion, were apparently mainly worn by women in the Migration Age. All bracteates were manufactured between 450 and 550 CE.

45 We must restrict ourselves scientifically to men only, because for the first several centuries of runic history, only men are recorded as having carved runic inscriptions, or having known the runes. Only later did women start to learn them. The original reason for this is probably that the runes arose in a restricted society which was male only—e.g., a poetic fraternity and/or a warrior band.

46 The idea of using the entire rune-row for magical purposes is recorded from the earliest times. For a catalog of these inscriptions see Flowers, *Runes and Magic* (Rûna-Raven, 2010, pp. 183–84 *et passim*).

47 The best known of these walking corpses are the *draugar* (sing. *draugr*) found in Icelandic lore. They are walking corpses, later called "ghosts," also.

48 Ibn Fadlan reports that a Rûs informed him that bodies are burned so that they "enter paradise immediately." See Ibn Fadlan (1998), p. 12.

49 The idea was that they were to "enjoy" the grave and not want to roam.

50   In the older runic period this was perhaps the main func-
     tion of runestones of any size. The mere presence of the
     stone, with its signs unintelligible to the masses, would
     cause fear in the minds of most.

51   This inscription is treated more fully in the article "On
     Magical Runes" by Magnus Olsen, which appears in
     translation in the first issue of *Symbel*. Its standard edi-
     tion is found in DR 311.

52   See Flowers, *Runes and Magic*, pp. 176–79.

53   See the *Egil's Saga* ch. 57.

54   Niding poetry, ON *nið*, is a satirical and insulting verse
     directed at one's political or religious enemies. These were
     often directed toward the clergy in the early phases of the
     Christianization process in Norway and Iceland.

55   The words *minni* and *minne* are based on the root mean-
     ing "memory," and this memory of the beloved is in the
     Germanic mind the essence of spiritual love.

56   This mandate was magically instilled in the Leira Working
     which was performed at that site in the summer of 2000.

57   See Flowers, *The Galdrabók*, and Thorsson, *Northern
     Magic*, pp. 121ff.

58   This is clearly attested to and proven by the texts repro-
     duced in *The Galdrabók* (Rûna-Raven, 2005).

59   This region is just north of Uppsala.

60   For a general outline of the runic philosophy of Johan Bure, see Flowers, *Johannus Bureus and the Adalruna* (Rûna-Raven, 1998).

61   A basic history of the renewal of the Rune-Gild in the past few decades is recorded in *History of the Rune-Gild* vol. III, published privately.

62   The Traditionalism of Evola and his school concentrates on the idea of a transcendental set of values or principles which constitute the Tradition, regardless of whether it has been passed down or not.

63   The Latin word *traditio*, from which we get the word "tradition," is based on the verb *trado*, which means "to hand or pass over."

64   *Rūnō* is mythically referred to as a feminine entity because it is a grammatically feminine word in the early Germanic languages.

65   Herman Te Velde in his article "The God Heka in Egyptian Theology" outlines this idea on a theoretical basis.

66   The Armanen system is still cultivated in the *Guido von List Gesellschaft* and *Armenen Orden* in Germany, and among a group called the Knights of Runes here in the United States, but for the most part even in Germany the more traditional fuþarks have come to the forefront in practical work today.

67   The Uthark system is extensively discussed in the works of Sigurd Agrell and has been most recently reintroduced

by Thomas Karlsson in his book *Uthark*. I have discussed the theory in an essay printed in *Green Rûna* (pp. 18–21), and it also plays a part in my work *The Tarok of the Magians* (Rûna-Raven, 2006).

68   Most of the known older inscriptions were collected and edited by Wolfgang Krause (1966).

69   The words "diachronic resonance" reflect a powerful idea and philosophy: that resonance from one pattern to another can take place diachronically, i.e., "through time." In this way, an act performed today can resonate with one performed in ages past, and one can be seen to affect the other.

70   This system follows that of Einar Haugen (*The Scandinavian Languages*, p. 119).

71   For a convenient edition of the OERP with a complete glossary of Old English words, see Flowers (*The Rune-Poems*, 2002).

72   The most complete discussion of runic manuscripts is provided by René Derolez in his *Runica Manuscripta* (1954).

73   The article in which these rules were outlined was translated in *Symbel* 1 (2006).

74   This is most interestingly illustrated in chapter 72 of *Egil's Saga* where Egill has to scrape away and neutralize an inscription made by another, less able, runemaster. The work was intended to heal a girl, but only made her worse due to mistakes in the formula. Luckily Egill is there to correct the error.

75   This is the principle used by Lee Hollander in his translation of the *Poetic Edda*; it was also a virtual "cause" in late Victorian England, where there was an effort to preserve and restore Anglo-Saxonisms in the current speech.

76   The rune-names themselves will be the subject of a forthcoming monograph to be published by Rûna-Raven in partnership with the Woodharrow Institute.

77   The *málrúnakenningar* are a series of kennings which refer to letters, usually referred to as "magical letters" known in Icelandic books of magic. These are collected and translated in Flowers, *The Rune-Poems* (Rûna-Raven, 2002), pp. 54–70.

78   The original Latin of this passage by Caesar reads: VI 28 *Tertium est genus eorum, qui uri appellantur. Hi sunt magnitudine paulo infra elephantos, specie et colore et figura tauri. Magna vis eorum est et magna velocitas, neque homini neque ferae quam conspexerunt parcunt. Hos studiose foveis captos interficiunt. Hoc se labore durant adulescentes atque hoc genere venationis exercent, et qui plurimos ex his interfecerunt, relatis in publicum cornibus, quae sint testimonio, magnam ferunt laudem. Sed adsuescere ad homines et mansuefieri ne parvuli quidem excepti possunt. Amplitudo cornuum et figura et species multum a nostrorum boum cornibus differt. Haec studiose conquisita ab labris argento circumcludunt atque in amplissimis epulis pro poculis utuntur.*

79   The best example of the rune being associated with fire is found in the OIRP, where we see it is given the kenning *flæðar viti*, "fire-beacon of the flood-tide." This indicates

a fire built on a seaside hilltop to act as a "lighthouse" for ships.

80 See Flowers, *The Rune-Poems* (pp. 20; 24; 63–70).

81 See Jan de Vries, *Altnordisches etymologisches Wörter-buch*, p. 20.

82 Myths of this kind are recorded in the Indo-Iranian world (i.e., in the eastern Indo-European realm) in which the gods/heroes Indra (in India) and Verethragna (in Iran) perform these kind of deeds.

83 See *The Rune Poems*, p. 64.

84 See Thorsson, *Runelore*, pp. 188–89.

85 See Streitberg, p. 112.

86 See Simek, p. 88.

87 See La Farge, p. 207.

88 This is attested, for example, in *Egil's Saga*, chapter 72.

89 See Jordanes, *History of the Goths* (XII: 78). This text is edited by Mierow (1960).

90 This concept is powerfully illustrated in a manuscript from the Middle Ages which shows the god Woden breathing fire into the mouths of the Anglo-Saxon kings. See Thorsson, *Green Rûna*, pp. 49–50.

91 Modern theories of evolution are merely the old traditions dressed up in scientific jargon. Likewise the current
craze about human beings created as a hybrid between
prehuman creatures and divine beings "from up there"
is a similar case of an old tradition being expressed in
terms that modernistic people can better understand. In
contrast to the sparse Old Testament lore in this regard,
the Norse tradition is extensive and elaborated on, see the
Eddic poems Völuspá and Rígsþula.

92 The standard edition of this artifact is provided by Krause
(1966), pp. 69–72.

93 See Flowers, *The Galdrabók*, p. 55.

94 This theme is discussed in my book *Sigurðr* (Rûna-Raven,
2011), *passim*.

95 See Bosworth and Toller, p. 150.

96 The Greek term *technē* originally referred to the ability to
use fire.

97 Mythically this is attested to in an Eddic passage, Völuspá
st. 24.

98 See Bosworth and Toller, p. 1285.

99 See Chisholm, pp. 49–50.

100 For a semiotic treatment of this inscription, see my article
"How to Do Things with Runes" (2006).

101 See Flowers, *The Galdrabók*, p. 55.

102 See Thorsson, *Runelore*, pp. 87–91.

103 For more about yew lore, see Ralph Elliott's article "Runes, Yews and Magic."

104 80. See Jan de Vries, *Altnordisches etymologisches Wörterbuch*, p. 20.

105 Myths of this kind are recorded in the Indo-Iranian world (i.e., in the eastern Indo-European realm) in which the gods/heroes Indra (in India) and Verethragna (in Iran) perform these kind of deeds.

106 See Cleasby-Vigfusson, p. 126.

107 See Thorsson, *Runelore*, pp. 188–89.

108 See Cleasby-Vigfusson, p. 579.

109 See Dickins, pp. 18–19.

110 This process is described in the Völuspá, stanzas 17–18.

111 Man does become the object of culture when it comes to practices of marriage and governance of the production of offspring. In the ancient Germanic culture, many tribes had rules about the production of offspring which seem to have bordered on a eugenic model. However, given their traditional anthropology, these rules may have been just as "spiritual" as they seem to be biological. The whole point was to help ensure healthy offspring with known biological and spiritual heritages.

112   See de Vries, pp. 373–74.

113   See Chisholm, *passim*.

114   See Lee M. Hollander, *The Poeta Edda* (1972), pp. 83–89.

115   See Simek, p. 260.

116   See de Vries, II: 167.

117   See Cleasby-Vigfusson, pp. 94–95; 112.

118   See Simek, p. 55.

119   Linguistically there were dialectic variants involving OE [ks] alternating with [sk] so that we see [fisk] and [fish]; *ascian* and *axian* (to ask), etc.

120   See Cleasby-Vigfusson p. 687.

121   See my article "The Holy," in *Green Rûna*, pp. 41–45.

122   See Chisholm, p. 52.

123   See Grimm I: 171, IV: 1479.

124   See Grimm I: 73–74.

125   See Cleasby-Vigfusson p. 25.

126   See Streitberg, p. 112.

127   See Simek, p. 88.

128 See *The Rune-Poems*, p. 43.

129 See Snorri, *Edda*, chapters 16–17.

130 See La Farge, p. 207.

131 See Cleasby-Vigfusson, p. 329.

132 See *Mysteries of the Goths*, pp. 101–8.

133 Besides *Runes and Magic* (1986; 2010), there have also been two articles, "A Semiotic Theory of Rune Magic," printed in *Studia Germanica* (Rûna-Raven, 2000) and "How to Do Things with Runes" (2006). The last of these was based on a paper I delivered at the Fifth International Symposium on Runes and Runic Inscriptions at Jelling, Denmark in the year 2000.

134 This is attested to, for example, in *Egil's Saga*, chapter 72.

135 See Wax and Wax (1962), pp. 180–82.

136 See Grambo (1975).

137 See Jordanes, *History of the Goths* (XII: 78). This text is edited by Mierow (1960).

138 See van Baal (1971), pp. 240–41.

139 Van Baal 1971: 263.

140 Tambiah (1973), p. 221.

141 Tambiah (1973), p. 199.

142 See Grambo (1975), p. 81.

143 This concept is powerfully illustrated in a manuscript from the Middle Ages which shows the god Woden breathing fire into the mouths of the Anglo-Saxon kings. See Thorsson, *Green Rûna*, pp. 49–50.

144 See Mindy MacLeod, *Bind-Runes* (2002).

145 See Flowers, *The Galdrabók*, p. 25 and Thorsson, *Northern Magic*, pp. 133–37.

146 Modern theories of evolution are merely the old traditions dressed up in scientific jargon. Likewise the current craze about humans being created as a hybrid between prehuman creatures and divine beings "from up there" is a similar case of an old tradition being expressed in terms that modernistic people can better understand. In contrast to the sparse Old Testament lore in this regard, the Norse tradition is extensive and elaborated, see the Eddic poems Völuspá and Rígsþula.

147 The standard edition of this artifact is provided by Krause (1966), pp. 69–72.

148 The clearest explanation of the lore of the Icelandic *landvættir* is contained in the Óláfs saga Tryggvasonar (chapter 33) which is found in the *Heimskringla* corpus.

149 See Flowers, *The Galdrabók*, p. 55.

150 This theme is discussed in my book *Sigurðr* (Rûna-Raven, 2011), *passim*.

151 This can be interpreted as a final younger **R**-rune or a mirror image of the older Υ-rune.

152 The Greek term *technē* originally referred to the ability to use fire.

153 This is seen in several examples in *The Galdrabók*.

154 This is found in the Sigrdrífumál (stanza 18) where it is said that the runes are carved, scraped off, and then blended with holy mead.

155 Egill, and many other skalds lived in the ninth century, composed poetry in a time when there was no other writing known to them and their contemporaries except runes. The poems were not committed to writing until some three to four centuries after their deaths. The only way these could have been kept alive is by memorization and traditional transmission of these verbatim works from one poet to the other.

156 See Ibn Fadlan, p. 12.

157 For an outline of runic divinatory practices, see Thorsson, *Runecaster's Handbook*, 1988.

158 This article was printed in *Mainstays* (Rûna-Raven, 2006), pp. 24–27.

159 See for example the article "Runes, Yews and Magic" by Ralph Elliott in *Speculum* 32, pp. 250–61.

160 See *The Rune-Poems* by S. E. Flowers (Rûna-Raven, 2002).

161 See Cross and Slover, p. 28.

BIBLIOGRAPHY

Austin, J. L. *How to Do Things with Words*. (The William James Lectures 1955) Oxford: Clarendon Press, 1962.

Baal, J. van. *Symbols for Communication: An Introduction to the Anthropological Study of Religion*. Assen: Van Gorrcum, 1971.

Bosworth, Joseph, and T. Northcote Toller. *An Anglo-Saxon Dictionary*. Oxford: Oxford University Press, 1898.

Byock, Jess, trans. *The Saga of the Volsungs*. London: Penguin, 1999.

Chisholm, James. *Grove and Gallows*. Smithville: Rûna-Raven, 2002.

Cleasby, Richard, and Gudbrand Vigfússon, eds. *An Icelandic-English Dictionary*. Oxford: At the Clarendon Press, 1957, 2nd ed.

Cross, Tom P., and Clark H. Slover, eds. *Ancient Irish Tales*. Dublin: Figgis, 1936.

Dickins, Bruce, ed. *Runic and Heroic Poems of the Old Teutonic Peoples*. Cambridge: Cambridge University Press, 1915.

Dillmann, François-Xavier. *Les magiciens dans l'Islande ancienne*. Diss. doctorat d'Etat. University of Caen, Caen, 1986.

Dumézil, Georges. *Gods and Myths of the Ancient Northmen*. Edited by Einar Haugen. Berkeley: University of California Press, 1973.

Elliott, Ralph. *Runes: An Introduction*. New York: St. Martins Press, 1989, 2nd ed.

———. "Runes, Yews and Magic." *Speculum* 32 (1957): 250–61.

Ellis (Davidson), H. R. *The Road to Hel*. Cambridge: Cambridge University Press, 1943.

Ellis Davidson, H. R. *Gods and Myths of Northern Europe*. Harmondsworth, UK: Penguin, 1964.

Finnegan, Ruth. "How to Do Things with Words: Performative Utterances among the Limba of Sierra Leone." *Man* *N.S.* 4 (1969): 537–52.

Flowers, Stephen E. "How to Do Things with Runes." In *Runes and Their Secrets*, edited by Marie Stoklund, et al. Copenhagen: Museum Tusculanum Press, 2006.

———. *Johannes Bureus and Adalruna*. Smithville: Rûna-Raven, 1998.

———. *The Magian Tarok*. Smithville: Rûna-Raven, 2006.

————. "Magic." In *Medieval Scandinavia: An Encyclopedia* edited by P. Pulsiano et al., 399–400. New York: Garland, 1993.

————. *Rúnarmál I*. Smithville: Rûna-Raven, 1996.

————. *The Rune-Poems*. Smithville: Rûna-Raven, 2002.

————. *Runes and Magic*. New York: Lang, 1986.

————. *Runes and Magic*. Smithville: Rûna-Raven, 2010, 3rd ed.

Grambo, Ronald. "Models of Magic." *Norveg* 18 (1975): 77–109.

Grimm, Jacob. *Teutonic Mythology*. Translated by S. Stallybrass. New York: Dover, 1966, 4 vols.

Grönbech, Vilhelm. *The Culture of the Teutons*. London: Oxford University Press, 1931.

Haugen, Einar. *The Scandinavian Languages*. Cambridge, MA: Harvard University Press, 1976.

Hollander, Lee M., trans. *The Poetic Edda*. Austin: University of Texas Press, 1973, 2nd ed.

Ibn Fadlan. *The Travel Report of Ibn Fadlan as It Concerns the Scandinavian Rûs*. With commentary by Stephen E. Flowers. Smithville: Rûna-Raven, 1998.

Jones, Gwyn. *A History of the Vikings*. London: Oxford University Press, 1984, 2nd ed.

Krause, Wolfgang, and Herbert Jankuhn. *Die Runeninschriften im älteren Futhark*. Göttingen: Vandenhoek & Ruprecht, 1966.

La Farge, Beatrice, and Tucker, John. *Glossary to the Poetic Edda*. Heidelberg: Winter, 1992.

MacLeod, Mindy. *Bind-Runes*. Uppsala: Institutionen för nordiska språk, 2002.

Mierow, Charles C., ed. *The Gothic History of Jordanes*. New York: Barnes & Noble, 1960.

Pálsson, Hermann, and Paul Edwards, trans. *Egil's Saga*. Harmondsworth, UK: Penguin, 1976.

————, trans. *Eyrbyggja Saga*. Harmondsworth, UK: Penguin, 1976.

Polomé, Edgar C. "Beer, Runes and Magic." *Journal of Indo-European Studies* 24:1–2 (1996): 99–105.

————. "Notes sur le vocabulaire religieux du germanique 1. Runique alu." *La Nouvelle Clio* 6 (1954): 49–55.

Sæmundsson, Matthías Viðar. *Galdrar á Íslandi*. Oddi: Almenna Bókfélag, 1992.

Schneider, Karl. *Die germanischen Runennamen*. Meisenheim: Anton Hain, 1956.

Simek, Rudolf. *Dictionary of Northern Mythology*. Woodbridge: Brewer, 1993.

Simpson, Jacqueline. *Icelandic Folktales and Legends*. Berkeley: University of California Press, 1972.

———. *Legends of Icelandic Magicians*. Cambridge: Brewer, 1975.

Streitberg, Wilhelm. *Die gotische Bibel*. Heidelberg: Winter, 1919–28, 2 vols.

Sturluson, Snorri. *Edda*. Translated by Anthony Faulkes. London: Dent, 1987.

———. *Heimskringla*. Translated by Lee M. Hollander. Austin: University of Texas Press, 1962, 2nd ed.

Tacitus. *The Agricola and Germania*. Translated by H. Mattingly. Harmondsworth: Penguin, 1970.

———. *The Histories*. Translated by K. Wellesley. Harmondsworth: Penguin, 1975.

Tambiah, Stanley J. "Form and Meaning of Magical Acts: A Point of View." In *Modes of Thought*, edited by R. Horton. London: Faber & Faber, 1973.

———. "The Magical Power of Words." *Man N.S.* 3 (1968): 175–208.

Te Velde, Herman. "The God Heka in Egyptian Theology." *Jaarbericht van het Vooraziatisch-Egyptisch Genootschap "Ex Oriente Lux"* 21 (1969–70): 71–92.

Thorsson, Edred. *Futhark*. York Beach, ME: Weiser, 1984.

———. *Green Rûna*. Smithville: Rûna-Raven, 1996, 2nd ed.

———. *Runecaster's Handbook*. York Beach, ME: Weiser, 1988.

———. *Runelore*. York Beach, ME: Weiser, 1987.

Turville-Petre, E. O. G. *Myth and Religion of the North*. New York: Holt, Rinehart and Winston, 1964.

Vries, Jan de. *Altgermanische Religionsgeschichte*. Berlin: de Gruyter, 1956–57, 2 vols., 2nd ed.

———. *Altnordisches etymologisches Wörterbuch*. Leiden: Brill, 1961.

Wax, Murray, and Rosalie Wax. "The Magical Worldview." *Journal for the Scientific Study of Religion* 1 (1962): 179–88.

Wesche, Heinrich. *Die althochdeutsche Wortschatz im Gebiete des Zaubers und der Weissagung*. Halle/Saale: Niemeyer, 1940.

ABOUT THE AUTHOR

Edred Thorsson received his doctorate in Germanic languages and Medieval Studies from the University of Texas. He is a translator of Guido von List's *The Secret of Runes*, and a former university professor of humanities. He is the author of the bestselling *Futhark: A Handbook of Rune Magic* and *Runelore*. Thorsson lives in Texas, where he practices rune magic.

TO OUR READERS